World Hunger

Edited by Claire Stanford

Editorial Advisor Lynn M. Messina

The Reference Shelf
Volume 79 • Number 5

The H. W. Wilson Company
2007

The Reference Shelf

The books in this series contain reprints of articles, excerpts from books, addresses on current issues, and studies of social trends in the United States and other countries. There are six separately bound numbers in each volume, all of which are usually published in the same calendar year. Numbers one through five are each devoted to a single subject, providing background information and discussion from various points of view and concluding with a subject index and comprehensive bibliography that lists books, pamphlets, and abstracts of additional articles on the subject. The final number of each volume is a collection of recent speeches, and it contains a cumulative speaker index. Books in the series may be purchased individually or on subscription.

Library of Congress has cataloged this serial title as follows:

World hunger / edited by Claire Stanford.
    p. cm —(Reference shelf ; v. 79, no. 5)
    Collection of articles reprinted from various journals and newspapers.
    ISBN 978-0-8242-1071-7 (alk. paper)
    1. Famines. 2. Food supply. 3. Hunger—Prevention. 4. Food relief. I. Stanford, Claire.
      HC79.F3W65 2007
      363.8—dc22

                                        2007034912

Cover: Iraqis on line to receive food aid at a mosque in Baghdad. (Photo by Karim Sahib/AFP/Getty Images)

Visit H. W. Wilson's Web site: www.hwwilson.com

Printed in the United States of America

The Reference Shelf®

1/09

Contents

Preface

The struggle to end world hunger has long been a subject of international attention and discourse. In 1948 the United Nations adopted the Universal Declaration of Human Rights, which enumerated, among other inalienable rights, the right to food. More than half a century later, in 2000, the United Nations again focused on hunger in its Millennium Declaration, which listed eight goals that UN member nations hoped to achieve by 2015. Chief among these objectives is cutting in half the number of people around the world who suffer from hunger.

Chronic hunger afflicts approximately 820 million people worldwide, killing 25,000 people every day, one child every eight seconds. While Asia has the largest number of people who are undernourished, the problem is most severe in Africa, particularly sub-Saharan Africa. In Asia and the Pacific region, 525 million people suffer from chronic hunger—17 percent of a total population of 3 billion. But conditions there are slowly improving. In sub-Saharan Africa, one out of every three people is undernourished, and the situation is unlikely to improve in the near future.

World hunger is such a difficult problem to address because so many equally intractable dilemmas contribute to it. Natural disaster, war, disease, lack of education, repressive gender roles, and political corruption all play a part in perpetuating the cycle. While it is perhaps universally accepted that hunger and famine must be counteracted, no consensus has yet emerged as to how best to do so. Compounding the problem is the considerable financial investment that any proposed solution would require. As the drive to end hunger stagnates, relief agencies fear that citizens of developed nations are becoming increasingly desensitized to famine's toll. Paradoxically, the more hunger there is in the world, the more normal—and less urgent—famines seem. However, given the increasingly globalized and technologically advanced state of the world, the problem of hunger is all the more abnormal and all the more urgent today.

This book examines the complex scientific, economic, political, and sociological aspects of world hunger by looking at the varied causes of famine—as well as their potential solutions. The articles in this book also give examples of famine's many different manifestations around the world. Selections in the first chapter, "The Slow and Silent Killer: What Causes Famine?" offer a theoretical overview of the various factors that contribute to famine, explaining each within the larger context of world hunger. Focusing on Niger, Kenya, Ethiopia, Malawi, Zimbabwe, and North Korea, articles in the next chapter, "Famines in the World Today," discuss the specific causes and effects of some of the most severe food shortages in recent years.

The third chapter, "Relief Efforts: Aid Versus Development," features entries that explore the difficulties relief agencies and governments face in providing immediate famine relief as well as their struggle to transition toward working on long-term development. While women and children are famine's principal and most visible victims, they are also envisioned as emerging leaders in the fight to end hunger, as selections in the next chapter, "Women and Children: Greatest Victims, Greatest Hope," demonstrate.

The controversial idea of biotechnology has recently entered the discussion about hunger. The science behind genetically modified crops and the arguments for and against them are explained in articles in the fifth chapter, "Promising Solution or Risky Experiment: The Biotechnology Debate." Finally, entries in the last chapter of the book, "Food Stamps and Farm Subsidies: Hunger in America," look at hunger in the United States, one of the wealthiest and most powerful nations in the world, where approximately 37 million people nonetheless do not have food security.

The appendix contains the text of the United Nations Millennium Declaration, which was adopted by the General Assembly in September 2000. The Declaration delineates the eight Millennium Development Goals, which include not only the aforementioned objective of halving world hunger by 2015, but also related goals concerning education, disease prevention, and empowerment of women.

I would like to thank the writers and publishers who have granted permission to reprint their work. In addition, I would especially like to thank Lynn Messina, Rich Stein, and Paul McCaffrey for their invaluable assistance.

Claire Stanford
October 2007

I. THE SLOW AND SILENT KILLER: WHAT CAUSES FAMINE?

Editor's Introduction

The exact cause of famine is clear: In certain regions of the world, people simply do not have enough food. But why is food scarce in some areas and not others? And why is food scarce at some times and not others? Why do some countries have severe but temporary famines while others suffer equally debilitating chronic food shortages? The articles in this chapter seek to answer these questions by exploring both the direct and indirect causes of hunger, which range from war to disease to the lack of initiative on the part of developed nations in putting an end to this crisis.

Susan Sechler discusses all of these possible causes in her article, "Starved for Attention," the first piece in this chapter. Sechler argues that the United States, as a powerful, wealthy nation, has a particular responsibility to prevent international famine; furthermore, she adds that following the September 11, 2001, terrorist attacks, it is in America's interest to better its image abroad, if only for purposes of national security. Sechler specifically looks at three regions of the world—China, Africa, and Bangladesh—and examines what techniques for preventing famine have and have not worked in each. She concludes with an eight-point plan for eradicating world hunger.

In the following article, "How the World Is Getting Hungrier Each Year," Paul Vallely also profiles specific regions of the world, giving brief descriptions of three countries where the food supply is improving and three countries where the situation is declining. He also more broadly discusses a report by the Food and Agriculture Organization (FAO) detailing these trends.

Stijn Claessens and Erik Feijen discuss the economics of famine in the next piece, "From Credit to Crops." The economists present the results of their study relating investment in agricultural equipment to financial development, financial development to agricultural productivity, and agricultural productivity to general nourishment. They conclude that even a small increase in a developing nation's private credit can go a long way toward decreasing the country's hunger.

In the subsequent piece, "Africa Needs Democracy as Much as Debt Relief," Steve Karlen argues that while debt relief may help alleviate hunger and poverty on the continent, it does not address the problem of political corruption, which he see as the major cause of Africa's woes. Though he acknowledges that debt relief may indeed be necessary, Karlen contends that fostering open and accountable government is even more essential if the continent is to emerge from its malaise.

The final two articles in this chapter present contrasting views on the impact of politics on food security. Both articles refer to the theory by Nobel Prize–winning economist Amartya Sen that democratic nations should not suffer from famine. Sen has reasoned that a democratically elected government would be more motivated to prevent famine than a dictatorship because the former would need to worry about its reelection; democracies also have a much freer flow of media and greater public discourse, making their governments further accountable. In "Why Democracies Don't Have Famines," Miren Gutierrez details the immediate causes of hunger-such as fighting, natural disasters, and political strife—while ultimately pointing the finger at the underlying inequalities in famine-stricken societies. In the chapter's final article, "Freedom Is Not Enough," Joshua Hammer takes the opposite stance, pointing to Malawi as evidence of a country suffering despite its democratic form of government. Hammer does note Sen's distinction between "functioning democracies" and "nonfunctioning democracies," of which Malawi is clearly the latter. Nevertheless, Hammer shows that the solution to world hunger is not as easy as simply creating a technically democratic government.

Starved for Attention

By Susan Sechler
The American Prospect, Winter 2002

As the aftermath of September 11 prompts questioning about anti-Western rage, a good starting point is a statistic: 800 million. That's the number of people in the developing countries who lack "food security"—who don't have enough food to perform the basic tasks of daily living. Of course, every American knows that there are millions of starving people in the world, but hunger has been such a constant and apparently insoluble fact of life for so long that few of us realize we have the means to end it—and have had for some time.

Nearly 30 years ago, U.S. Secretary of State Henry Kissinger made a promise to the first World Food Conference: "Within a decade, no child will go to bed hungry." No one has made good on Kissinger's promise, but he was correct that it was possible. We had the means; we lacked the motivation. After September 11, we have both. If moral concern alone is not enough to impel serious U.S. action on reducing world hunger, our national interest—and national security—certainly ought to be. Happily, national interest and moral responsibility coincide here. As a primary beneficiary of economic globalization and one of its principal rule-makers, the United States has a special responsibility to build a world market that works against hunger. And while it is clear that the multimillionaire Osama bin Laden was not even pretending to act on behalf of the poor and hungry, the surprising outpouring of anti-American bile we've seen from parts of the third world these last few months surely owes much to the problems of poverty and hunger. It is easy to hate a nation where food is wasted and more than 60 percent of the people are officially overweight (as defined by the U.S. Centers for Disease Control) when its leaders will not take significant steps to help the hungry.

So far, American policy makers have been too preoccupied with defending the homeland and stimulating the economy to begin the process of thinking differently about how to approach food security. But our changed understanding of the American place in the world—our inescapable interdependence with and vulnerability to the rest of humanity—makes the problem of world hunger more urgent. Hunger is not new, but the worldwide flow of communications, ideas, capital, labor, and opportunity provides policy makers with ways to help poor people generate income in formerly remote areas. If we use the tools at our disposal to fight world hunger seriously, the benefits will redound to all of us—in the West and in the developing world—politically, economically, and morally.

Global Trade and World Hunger

The last decade was the richest in world history, so it seems reasonable that the proportion of people in developing countries who are undernourished dropped from 20 percent to 17 percent; that's 40 million fewer hungry people worldwide in 2000 than in 1990. But China alone accounted for 76 million fewer people going hungry—which means that in most other developing nations, hunger actually increased. Regionally, sub-Saharan Africa has the hardest time feeding itself, with 34 percent of the population, or 194 million people, going hungry. While "only" 16 percent of those in the Asia and Pacific regions are hungry, that's almost 500 million people. In Latin America, there are 53.6 million hungry people (11 percent of the population); in North Africa and the Middle East, 32.5 million (9 percent).

Three-fourths of the world's hungry are politically marginalized people who live in rural areas.

Power relationships tell us who is likely to be hungry. Three-fourths of the world's hungry are politically marginalized people who live in rural areas. Within the family, women and children are the most likely to go hungry. Studies have found that educating women is the most significant step in reducing hunger. Thus, in poor countries, any government like the Taliban that bans the education of women virtually guarantees child hunger.

Expanding trade has improved food security in countries that have been able to take advantage of it. Economists at the International Food Policy Research Institute (IFPRI) measure a country's food security in a combination of ways: domestic production, nutritional status of the most vulnerable, education levels, and the percentage of export earnings that a country uses to import food. Before the explosion of the global food market in the early 1970s, this export/import percentage was fairly uniform across countries, ranging between 15 and 20 percent. By 1998 the average had dropped substantially, to 6 percent—but for the least developed countries, where growth in exports has been substantially slower than the aggregate growth of trade, the percentage is up, closer to 23 percent.

Any number of reasons can account for why poorer countries have to spend so much of their export money on food, but unfair trade practices imposed by first-world countries is a big one. Many poor nations face market barriers to their goods abroad—on everything from textiles to sugar—while their farmers at home must compete with highly subsidized food and agricultural goods from the world's richest nations in North America and Europe.

The Uruguay Round of trade negotiations from 1986 to 1994 was meant to lower these rich-country subsidies; it largely failed. Wealthy countries—members of the Organization for Economic Cooperation and Development (OECD)—have continued to subsidize their domestic farmers' production at a rate of $365 billion a year. (Total official development assistance, meanwhile, has been running at about $55 billion yearly.) Buoyed by these subsidies, farm production in the United States and other OECD countries has increased steadily, depressing world prices, discouraging producers in developing countries, and putting valuable trade earnings out of the reach of the poorest countries. The effect is that poor countries get cheap food dumped on them from the subsidized farmers in the United States and elsewhere. Little of this imported food gets to the hungry in the countryside; most winds up with the urban elite. This is clearest in Africa, where the better-off in the seaport capitals can be fed more cheaply by subsidized U.S. and European grain than by food trucked hundreds of miles over bad roads from the interior. Thus, the middle class in Dakar, Senegal, eat baguettes made of wheat, while up-country farmers go broke and hungry for lack of markets.

Of course, the United States has a duty to take care of its own small farmers. But its agricultural subsidies go to only one-third of U.S. farmers, while two-thirds of the money goes to the largest and richest 10 percent of those eligible. Moreover, this puts the nation's agricultural policy, foreign policy, and development policy at three-way cross-purposes. In October the United States was following several contradictory courses simultaneously: trying to bring poor Asian nations into its coalition against terror; participating in agenda drafting for a new round of trade negotiations in Doha, Qatar, aimed largely at getting rid of domestic farm subsidies; and working on legislating a farm bill that called for $171 billion to be paid over the next 10 years to mainly wealthy farmers (who in turn donate to the politicians who fight for their subsidies). The aggregate effect of all these conflicting impulses is to make a hash of U.S. food-security policy.

America's Flawed Food Policy

In 1948, the United Nations Universal Declaration of Human Rights proclaimed that access to food is a human right. The United States agreed—until recently. At the 1996 World Food Summit, we changed our position on this basic right, reportedly for fear of legal implications. Moreover, U.S. aid to foreign countries is low compared with other OECD countries in terms of percentage of gross domestic product—in fact, it is the lowest, at one-tenth of 1 percent of GDP—and most of the aid we do provide goes to a few better-off countries, primarily Israel and Egypt. How can we be taken seriously when we say, as we often do, that we want to work with partners to improve global food security if we refuse to provide resources and are afraid to acknowledge food security as a basic human right?

The primary U.S. international food-assistance program, Food for Peace, is dramatically out of sync with the times. Since its inception in the 1950s, reform compromises have left a bureaucratic nightmare—a Rube Goldberg device rigged around and through a maze of politically tendentious government agencies, including the Department of Agriculture, the State Department, USAID, the Office of Management and Budget, the National Security Council, and even the Treasury. With such a cumbersome and conflicted system, it is hardly surprising that after a decision was made to provide emergency food relief for Afghanistan, delivery was held up for days while U.S. government officials argued about whether the food would be bought in the United States or in Pakistan.

Worse, the program's resources are still tilted toward moving U.S. farm surpluses into export markets rather than feeding hungry people. Title I of Food for Peace benefits American farmers by providing loans for the purchase of U.S. agricultural commodities to be used as food aid. The program's budget was increased by 50 percent in 1998—despite repeated reports from the General Accounting Office and elsewhere that the effort is of little help in market development or to the poor. Meanwhile, the budget for Title II—under which food is given to non-governmental organizations for humanitarian distribution—was increased only marginally, after having been allowed in the past to fall below the amount required by law. The budget of Title III, a government-to-government program aimed at encouraging development, has fared even worse: It has shrunk from $300 million in 1993 to $30 million in 2001.

To be fair, it should be noted that the United States is the biggest donor to the UN World Food Program and that our contributions rise as our surpluses do. This food is mostly for emergency relief, which is no bad thing. But we devote insufficient food aid to the fight against chronic hunger. We refuse to recognize the benefits we would reap if, as the world's richest superpower, we put a higher political priority on assuring food security for the world's poor and less on the demands of the farm lobby.

Lessons from China

As mentioned, China has reduced the number of its hungry by 76 million since 1990. Are there lessons from the Chinese example that could be applied elsewhere—or is China unique?

The answer is mixed. On the one hand, China's example demonstrates that independent government action can produce rapid results. On the other, few developing countries duplicate China's precise set of circumstances: a strong government, a commitment to improving small-scale farming and rural enterprise, an entrepreneurial population, a decent infrastructure, and a high population density that makes it easier to get food to markets—an advantage Africa notably lacks. China, unlike Africa, was able to take advantage of "Green Revolution" crops, mainly rice and wheat, and it has been developing its own biotech crops. It opened food markets a bit, a step popular with farmers. And it relied not on foreign capital but, rather, on the creation of credit domestically. (China now has a savings rate of almost 40 percent of GDP, and the second-largest capital reserves in the world.)

Globalization has also helped China—although its leaders have insisted on defining the terms. In 1978, when the new regime opened its doors to the West, a flood of

> While most of the world's hungry live in Asia, hunger is most intractable in Africa.

scientific and political ideas came in, further stimulating an already highly innovative population to produce more. But information now flows out of as well as into China—and as the economist Amartya Sen has demonstrated, famine does not occur where information travels freely. It is thus improbable that 30 million Chinese people will starve to death as they did in the 1958–1961 famines.

But China's refusal to bow to demands for globalization on Western terms will not be easy for poorer countries, especially small ones, to emulate. China controls its own currency, so it is not prey to global financial speculators and the International Monetary Fund. And the country's mixture of authoritarian government and market enterprise has allowed it to open itself up only to the degree that Beijing judges beneficial. It's unlikely that this style of authoritarian state capitalism could work elsewhere in the world.

Africa Still Starves

While most of the world's hungry live in Asia, hunger is most intractable in Africa. More than three-fourths of Africans are farmers, and three-fourths of these farmers are women, many of them struggling alone to support their families, with husbands off trying to find work in the cities or dead or dying of AIDS. Some 90 percent of Africa's hungry are rural; but since the continent's political elite tend to live in port cities, the rural areas suffer government neglect. As an aid worker remarked during the 1984–1985 African famine: "Starve the city people and they riot; starve the rural people and they die. If you were an African political leader, which would you choose?" Thus, leaders skew policies toward city folk to the detriment of the vast majority of their people. Droughts may trigger famines in Africa, but their deeper underlying causes lie in the political choices of African governments and the slow response to these emergencies by food-giving governments.

Ineffective or unjust governments also cause wars. According to IFPRI, there have been 17 major armed conflicts in Africa over the past decade (in the same period, the entire rest of the world had 10). The use of hunger as an active weapon in these conflicts has left nearly 20 million people, most of them women and children, in need of food and humanitarian assistance. For a continent dependent on agricultural production for foreign exchange as well as sustenance, the longer-term effects of these conflicts are even more severe.

According to one UN estimate, Africa lost almost one-third of its agricultural production because of conflicts between 1970 and 1997. And globalization has not been much help to countries that cannot attract investment.

> History shows that U.S. intervention can make a huge difference in a nation's ability to feed itself.

Given that Africa's hungry are mainly small farmers working exhausted soil far from markets, ending hunger there will depend largely on increasing crop production on tiny farm lots. African farmers must acquire new techniques and technologies that rely on heavier use of chemical fertilizer as well as organic farming methods; most of Africa lacks sufficient natural material for an organic-only route, and few farmers can afford a chemical-fertilizer-only approach. The most effective technologies will be those that provide drought-tolerance and resistance to specific pests and diseases yet are inexpensive and tailored to African ecosystems.

Traditionally, many such advances have come from government-funded research in U.S. universities and from the 16 international research centers whose donors are coordinated by the World Bank. But budgets for research targeted at the needs of poor farmers have been allowed to stagnate and decline. The total budget of the 16 international centers is only a thousandth of what the OECD spends on farm subsidies. Biotechnology could help; for instance, drought-resistant crops may be just over the horizon. But most biotech research is moving away from such public-interest goals and toward private-sector needs. In its aggressive push to protect intellectual-property rights, the U.S. government provides patents for new biotech crop varieties without regard to the importance of these crops to poor countries or the deadening effect such policies have on locally tailored innovation. And even universities patent their discoveries now, usually providing exclusive licenses to the private sector rather than sharing them with other public institutions. These new practices, combined with corporate fearfulness of legal entanglements, have virtually halted the free flow of both the germ plasm necessary for crop development and the information critical to research for the hungry.

Success in Bangladesh

History shows that U.S. intervention can make a huge difference in a nation's ability to feed itself. Throughout the 1960s, stored U.S. grain surpluses served as a food safety net for the entire world. But in 1972, the United States made its first major grain sale to Russia, sharply drawing down its reserves and sending prices skyward. Bangladesh, fragile after flooding and war, could no longer afford grain at market prices. With U.S. food aid reduced, a crisis loomed. By 1974, on the eve of the first World Food Conference, Bangladesh was lurching toward a major famine. In making the argument to deny further aid, a high-ranking U.S. State Department official called the country "a basket case." (It is fair to note that the case was complicated by the fact that Bangladesh was trading with Cuba.)

Facing the outcry of the U.S. public and the international community, who were learning about the effects of the approaching famine from the media, Senators George McGovern and Dick Clark—in attendance at the Rome conference—prevailed on Earl Butz, the reluctant secretary of agriculture, to wire President Nixon asking him to reverse the U.S. policy and double aid to Bangladesh. The United States did—but not before more than 200,000 people starved to death.

The famine shocked the United States and its partners into action and the "basket case" assessment was proved wrong: The international community mounted a $30-billion broad-based effort at alleviating poverty and ensuring food security in Bangladesh. Since then, the country has become largely self-sufficient in rice and population growth rates have slowed. Though a third of the populace still suffer from food insecurity, the famines of only a few decades ago no longer threaten. If there is a lesson to be drawn from Bangladesh's example, it is that the U.S. government vastly underestimates what public action can achieve if it is broadly based, well provisioned, and organized around a clear and concrete goal like ending hunger.

An Eight-Point Plan for Feeding the World

Ending world hunger requires that the United States and its partners create a global marketplace in which producers from poor countries can compete fairly against those in industrialized nations. If we continue to support a market that favors the rich at the expense of the poor, we will continue to breed tension and turmoil in developing countries—and anger against the United States.

Most of the positive steps that must be taken to achieve global food security are well known. Most are political rather than technical, and many require the United States to work with other nations. Here's what our government must do.

- Secure the commitment of other countries and set the shared goal of completely ridding the planet of hunger by 2015—not just cutting it in half, as governments at the 1996 World Food Summit pledged to do. Then take whatever steps are necessary to complete the task.

- Agree that access to adequate food is a basic human right, so that broad-based international efforts by governments, nonprofits, and the business sector to build a safety net will have firm support. A global market needs a global safety net.

- Reform the protocols and agreements that apply to early intervention by the global community when conditions that spread world hunger begin to build. This will require a long-term plan for providing food to people marooned in war zones.

- Separate food assistance and other developmental aid from "America First" principles and bureaucratic squabbling—and emphasize support for nutrition programs targeted to women and children.

- Reduce the perverse subsidies to OECD-country farmers and remove trade barriers that hinder poor nations.

- Lead the developed countries in creating intellectual-property-rights regimes and institutional frameworks that will ensure a robust intellectual common for agricultural science. This will involve facilitating the exchange of germ plasm with poor countries, protecting genetic resources, strengthening farmers' rights, preventing exclusive licensing of so-called enabling technologies, and helping to build scientific capacity in Africa.

- Streamline the donor politics that surround the international research centers and increase the centers' resources so they can better support farmer-led innovation for the hungry in Africa.

- Most important, give the problem of world hunger the priority and attention it deserves so that we will not just try to address hunger effectively but will actually succeed.

The poor of the world cannot afford to have us do less. And now it's clear that the United States can't afford to do less either.

How the World Is Getting Hungrier Each Year

By Paul Vallely
The Independent (London), November 26, 2003

I have never forgotten my first experience of ordinary life in an African village. I had been in Ethiopia, covering the terrible famine of 1985, with its haunted lines of starving, blank-eyed faces, sitting waiting for death. But I had not been to an ordinary village.

Not long after, I travelled to Sudan where drought had also shrivelled the land. Halfway to the famine area our four-wheel-drive stopped to refuel. There by the roadside in the parched scrub was a dusty straw-thatched hut. Outside a family was huddled around a meagre fire made from a handful of sticks. The children had swollen bellies and thin limbs. The mother was cooking a single piece of flat bread which was the entire meal for the whole family. "Why didn't you tell me we were in the famine area already," I said to my guide.

He laughed. "That's not famine," he chided. "That's just ordinary life in Africa. Being hungry is normal."

The world is getting hungrier, according to a report issued by the United Nations food agency yesterday. After a decade of improvements for the planet's poor, things have taken a serious turn for the worst. Hunger, which fell steadily throughout the first half of the 1990s, is on the rise again.

Across the world an estimated 842 million people are today undernourished—and that figure is again climbing, with an additional 5 million hungry people every year. The figures, says the report by the Food and Agriculture Organisation (FAO) "signal a setback in the war on hunger." The prospect of cutting by half the number of people who go hungry—the target set by the world's governments in 1996—looks "increasingly remote."

The shocking thing about this is that, in the world of the politics of aid, at any rate, nobody is shocked.

The report tries to put on a brave face. "First some good news," it begins, reporting that the number of chronically hungry people has declined by 80 million in 19 countries, including Brazil, Chad, Guinea, Namibia and Sri Lanka.

So why is the picture so grim everywhere else? The number of those going hungry in India has risen by 19 million since 1995–97, and yet China has reduced its figure by 58 million since 1990–92. "We must ask ourselves why this has happened," says the FAO director-general, Jacques Diouf, in his introduction.

Those who have bucked the trend share five characteristics, he concludes—faster economic growth, rapid expansion in the agricultural sector, slower population growth, lower rates of HIV infection and far fewer natural emergencies.

> The economics of globalisation are that the very poorest get poorer still.

"The role of capital is decisive," said Hartwig de Haen, assistant director of the FAO's economic and social department in Washington. "Investment in agriculture is a precondition for growth in incomes of the poor and the food supply," he said.

Yet such investment has been declining. Rich countries must put more cash into the agriculture sectors of poor countries. It must, he said, "go back to the level where it was in the early Nineties."

If only it were so simple. The truth is that the 19 nations who have bucked the trend have not been the authors of their own good fortune.

They have been lucky not to have experienced the high levels of droughts and natural disasters that have increasingly afflicted the Third World over the past decade.

Nor have domestic politics had much influence over rates of population growth, which tend to be determined fairly directly by levels of poverty—the worse things are, the more children you need to look after you in your old age.

Nor have many poor nations been able to manage their Aids epidemics in the way the rich world has with its new drug regimes. It is easy for us in the First World to forget the scale of the ravages of Aids—which has killed some 25 million people in the poor world. In this decade it will claim more lives than all the world's wars and disasters of the past half-century. Aids takes a terrible economic toll; it kills off farmers in their prime and leaves behind young orphans and aged parents—mouths with no one to feed them.

Neither is it a coincidence that those countries most dependent on agriculture are those with the most hunger. Increasing the amounts of flowers and strawberries grown for export near Third World airports may help the balance of payments, but it does little for pastoral and subsistence agriculture in remoter rural areas. The economics of globalisation are that the very poorest get poorer still. There are some places to which wealth just never trickles down.

There is gloomy evidence of this in the report. "At least half the higher prices received for exports went not to farmers but traders," it notes, "and there was no increase in production in response to the higher prices." Worst still, it adds, "prices are expected to rise more steeply for food products that developing countries import than for the commodities they export.

"Overall," it predicts, "the lion's share of benefits from trade liberalisation is expected to go to developed countries."

An Undernourished Planet

Three Improving Countries

Brazil

Luiz Lula da Silva, the President, pledged to eradicate hunger by the end of his four-year term. The number of undernourished Brazilians has fallen from 12 per cent in 1990 to 9 per cent in 2000, thanks to food aid, more jobs and higher income from food production.

Bangladesh

Cyclone-plagued, flood-drenched, over-populated and penniless, Bangladesh was the international byword for disaster. But now, with higher remittances from manual workers in the Gulf and a booming garments industry, growth of more than 5 per cent is forecast next year.

Vietnam

In the past 20 years Vietnam has achieved what the UN calls "remarkable" success. In 1979 a third of the population was undernourished; now it is about one fifth. One of the biggest factors has been a national programme encouraging families to grow vegetables and fruit, combined with education on balanced meals.

Three Declining Countries

Guatemala

A combination of a weak economy perpetuated by years of political instability, a series of natural disasters, including hurricanes and droughts, and the belief among donors that poverty in Central America is not as bad as in Africa or Asia has left Guatemalans growing hungrier.

India

India reduced the number of malnourished people by 20 million from 1990–92 and 1995–97, but the number subsequently rose by 19 million. Population growth and unemployment often offset well-intentioned government programmes. Half of all children in India under four are malnourished.

North Korea

Struggling to recover from a famine in the mid-1990s caused by natural disasters and mismanagement. In 1990–92 18 per cent of the population was malnourished. By 2001 it was 34 per cent. About 6.5 million people will depend on aid to survive next year.

This will surprise no one. The report repeats the familiar statistic that the West spends 30 times more on domestic farming subsidies than it does on aid. It catalogues how the US spends $3.9bn (pounds 2.3bn) a year subsidising its 25,000 cotton farmers—more than the entire GDP for Burkina Faso where 2 million people depend on cotton for their livelihood. Europe is now the world's second-largest sugar exporter even though EU sugar costs twice as much to produce as does that of Third World peasants.

Yet the harsh truth is—as the failure of the World Trade Organisation round in Cancun brutally showed—the industrialised world has abandoned any pretence that trade negotiations are anything to do with development.

Set against the scale of such large problems and political intransigence, the triumphs the report charts are small by comparison.

In Brazil, President Lula da Silva has launched a Zero Hunger project, with electronic cash cards for needy families and subsidised food in schools, workplaces and "people's restaurants," all linked to work and literacy incentives. In Vietnam great steps forward have been taken through nutrition education with poor families being schooled in a "coloured bowl" to encourage the right mix of rice, vegetables, meat and fish. But in much of Africa and Latin America the wherewithal is not there for such schemes. It is there that the vast majority of those 842 million people go to bed hungry at night—though interestingly 34 million of them are in the former Soviet Union countries, and 10 million even in the rich industrialised world.

Halving hunger was not the only Millennium Development Goal agreed by the United Nations General Assembly in 1992. There were also to be swingeing attacks on child mortality, illiteracy and education discrimination against girls. There were targets on aid levels, environmental sustainability and creating greater access to world markets for the products of the poorest countries. On most of these the rich world's promises are slipping too.

"Bluntly stated," the report concludes, "the problem is not so much a lack of food as a lack of political will." Bluntly stated, the problem is that none of us really cares.

From Credit to Crops

By Stijn Claessens and Erik Feijen
Finance & Development, March 2007

Although most countries experienced healthy per capita growth rates in the 20th century, extreme poverty and undernourishment are still widespread. In 2001, GDP per capita was, on average, about $21 a day, but more than half the world's population lived on less than $2 a day and more than 1 billion lived on less than $1 a day. And in the late 1990s, on average, about 20 percent of the world's population was undernourished—ranging from a high of 70.5 percent in Eritrea to virtually zero in most developed countries. For the international community, both measures of development, or the lack thereof, are critical. They form the number one Millennium Development Goal for 2015: reducing income poverty by half and reducing hunger by half from their 1990 levels. One could even argue that reducing undernourishment should take priority, given that being undernourished—when an individual cannot obtain enough food to meet dietary energy requirements continuously—defines a person's chances of living.

For a long time, economists have known that higher growth and lower inequality reduce poverty and hunger. They have also known that a better financial sector helps growth and reduces inequality. And in recent years, studies have tied these together, showing that financial development reduces poverty. But does financial development also reduce hunger and, if so, how? Is it just because more developed countries tend to have better-developed financial systems and less undernourishment simultaneously? Or is it because financial sector development promotes economic growth, which reduces income poverty, allowing more people to eat better? Or is it because there are specific channels through which better financial services directly ameliorate undernourishment? The answers to these questions matter to the extent that they can help guide policy interventions aimed at greater financial sector development. We recently undertook a study (Claessens and Feijen, 2006) to explore these questions. Our findings suggest that increased agricultural productivity and investments in agricultural equipment hold the key.

Article by Stijn Claessens and Erik Feijen from *Finance & Development* March 2007, Vol. 44, No. 1, published and copyrighted by the International Monetary Fund. Reprinted with permission.

Finance-Poverty-Hunger Links

It is well understood why financial development helps alleviate poverty. If poor people have access to financial services, they can obtain funds to invest in productivity-enhancing assets, say, a small weaving machine. They can borrow to buy a shop or find capital to start a small firm. By accumulating financial assets and availing themselves of insurance, households can reduce the impact of such unfortunate events as drought, disease, or death, which are part of daily life in many developing countries. If households have better access to financing, a calamity need not force them to sell productive assets such as a cow or a tractor, keeping a bad situation from worsening dramatically. Instead, they can save for their old age.

How much does financial development reduce poverty? Recent research suggests that the impact is significant and of a causal nature. One study finds that a 10 percentage point increase in private credit as a percentage of GDP (*private credit*), a common proxy for financial development, reduces poverty ratios by 2.5–3.0 percentage points (Honohan, 2003). Another study shows that financial development actually accelerates poverty reduction (Beck, Demirgüç-Kunt, and Levine, 2005). For example, if between 1985 and 2000 Peru had improved its private credit from 13 percent to 54 percent, the level prevailing in Chile, 2 percent of Peruvians would have been living in poverty in 2000, rather than the actual 15 percent.

> Financial development can be expected to reduce hunger largely by reducing poverty.

Given the strong relationship between income poverty and hunger, and given that financial development reduces income poverty, financial development can be expected to reduce hunger largely by reducing poverty. There is ample country evidence that income poverty is the main cause of undernourishment. For example, in Indonesia during 1984–87, rising income standards reduced malnutrition, and the fraction of people living on fewer than 1,400 calories a day fell by 26 percent.

What might be the specific channels through which financial development affects hunger? In terms of indirect effects, financial sector development reduces income poverty, which would allow people to better satisfy their dietary needs. Financial sector development also would make it easier for households to smooth consumption, reducing the effects of adverse income shocks on undernourishment. In terms of direct effects, one would expect financial development to facilitate higher value added per agricultural worker. With better access to credit, farmers can acquire inputs and equipment—such as fertilizer, tractors, other farming equipment, and livestock—that make them more productive and enhance overall agricultural productivity. That, in turn, causes increased food output, improved household incomes, and lower food prices—reducing undernourishment.

Our study, which covered more than 50 countries between 1980 and 2003 (using data from World Bank, 2005), tried to find evidence of these channels. We analyzed three relationships: between financial development and overall agricultural productivity; between agricultural productivity and nourishment; and, most important, between financial sector development and investment in agricultural equipment. As part of a second round of testing, we related financial sector development to other productivity measures, such as crop and livestock production and cereal yields; checked whether cereal yield, a specific productivity measure, related positively to undernourishment; and explored whether financial sector development relates to the use of two productivity-enhancing inputs—fertilizer and tractor use.

Following other studies of the relationship between financial sector development and poverty, we proxied financial development by private credit, which is the value of credit extended by financial intermediaries to the private sector as a percentage of GDP. And we used several country-level control variables that are likely to affect these relationships. Specifically, we controlled for the initial level of undernourishment, government expenditures as a percentage of GDP, economic development, initial income poverty, inflation, the fraction of the population in rural areas, the fraction of the population employed in the agricultural sector, and openness of the country (the value of trade, exports plus imports, as a fraction of GDP). In some cases, we also took into account production and trade in food.

On the Hunger Front

Our results show that a 1 percent increase in private credit to GDP would reduce the prevalence of undernourishment by between 0.22 percent and 2.45 percent. By comparison, a 1 percent increase in GDP per capita would reduce the prevalence of undernourishment by about 0.85 percent. The impact of financial sector development on undernourishment is substantial—at a minimum, about one-fourth that of general development—implying that there is a lot to gain from financial sector development, especially because of its great potential to increase. The ratio of private credit to GDP in low-income countries, for example, is about 16 percent, well below the 88 percent level in high-income countries.

Not only does this indirect link between financial development and undernourishment remain statistically strong after we take into account other factors that are known to affect poverty and hunger; all analyses work even when they take into account the possibility that the relationship between hunger and financial development actually goes the other way: financial development occurs because better-nourished people are economically more active and have a higher demand for financial services. Although there undoubtedly is some reverse causality, the development of the financial sector is far more important to reducing hunger than is a decline in undernourishment to stimulating demand for financial services. Even when we take the redundant step of including poverty and GDP per capita, the effects of financial sector development on undernourishment remain significant at the 10 percent level.

How about any direct links? First, *we found evidence to support the causal link between private credit and agricultural productivity.* Our analysis implies that a 1 percent increase in private credit to GDP boosts value added per agricultural worker by 1.0–1.7 percent. We also found specific evidence of increases in crop yields, especially of cereals, and livestock production because of greater financial sector development. In both cases, the positive relationship continued after we controlled for the effect of several other factors that could drive the links.

Second, *we found a causal relationship between value added per agricultural worker and undernourishment.* For example, a 1 percent increase in value added per agricultural worker reduces the prevalence of undernourishment by 0.4–1.0 percent. We also found evidence that, as farmers become more productive, the increased

---

There is still much that is not known about how best to enhance access to financial services for the poor and undernourished.

---

food supply and lower prices benefit society as a whole, including people who are unable to obtain financial services themselves but can afford a better diet because food prices are lower.

Third, *we found evidence to support the important causal link between the financial sector and investment in agricultural equipment.* Our results imply that private credit is significantly associated with fertilizer use and the use of tractors per worker, even after we controlled for the initial level of fertilizer use, the use of tractors, GDP per capita, and poverty. We also found evidence that it is not just financial sector development itself that matters in reducing undernourishment, but also the ease of access to financial services. For example, the more banking branches there were per 1,000 square kilometers in 2003–04, the lower the level of undernourishment. This relationship held, even when we took into account trade activity, government size, inflation, and the fraction of people living in rural areas. We also found that reach matters for the various productivity measures.

Fostering Financial Development

Because financial sector development can play a significant role in reducing not only income poverty but also undernourishment, it can contribute substantially to attaining the number one Millennium Development Goal (Claessens and Feijen, 2007). Many policies could foster financial sector development, including ensuring a stable macroeconomic environment, enhancing financial sector regulation and supervision, creating a proper information institutional infrastructure, and enforcing property rights.

However, there is still much that is not known about how best to enhance access to financial services for the poor and undernourished. The formal financial system has had only a minimal relationship with extremely poor people in many developing countries. And microfinance institutions have a small presence in most countries. Still, mainstream commercial banks have begun to serve the lower market segment in some developing countries and other success stories are emerging, including the development of sustainable micro-finance institutions, such as Grameen Bank in Bangladesh, whose founder Muhmmad Yunus won the Nobel Peace Prize last year. Technology also appears to hold promise. If early experiences with mobile phone banking, smart cards, and extending credit on the basis of simple scoring models are prophetic, then these developments could facilitate the delivery of financial services to many more people at low cost.

References

Beck, Thorsten, Asli Demirgüç-Kunt, and Ross Levine, 2005, "Finance, Inequality and Poverty: Cross-Country Evidence," NBER Working Paper No. 10979 (Cambridge, Massachusetts: National Bureau of Economic Research).

Claessens, Stijn, and Erik Feijen, 2006, "Finance and Hunger: Empirical Evidence of the Agricultural Productivity Channel," World Bank Research Working Paper No. 4080 (Washington).

———, 2007, "Financial Sector Development and the Millennium Development Goals," World Bank Working Paper No. 89 (Washington).

Honohan, Patrick, 2003, "Financial Development, Growth and Poverty: How Close Are the Links?" World Bank Policy Research Working Paper No. 3203 (Washington).

World Bank, 2005, *World Development Indicators* (Washington).

Africa Needs Democracy as Much as Debt Relief

BY STEVE KARLEN
THE CAPITAL TIMES (MADISON, WISCONSIN), JULY 27, 2005

Despite all of the publicity this month's Live 8 concerts generated for poverty in Africa, liberals and conservatives alike have failed to devise any kind of meaningful strategy for the troubled continent.

"Something must be done, even if it doesn't work," said Live 8 promoter Bob Geldof.

While Geldof certainly means well, good intentions are far too little and much too late on a continent in the midst of its fifth straight decade of descent into famine, disease and violence. Efforts in Africa must be judged by results. Without an emphasis on success, any action merely continues the visionless policy toward Africa that Geldof and his allies seek to correct.

Since Africa achieved independence in the 1960s, international organizations such as the International Monetary Fund and the World Bank have granted African nations loans on the condition that they make adjustments to their economies. These adjustments included limits on government spending.

Unfortunately, these efforts failed. Education and medical services became the first casualties of spending limits, further deteriorating living conditions. Not only did World Bank and IMF loans create enormous debt, they left Africa perpetually dependent on foreign aid.

Dropping the debt is not necessarily a bad idea. Compounding interest makes it virtually impossible for many countries to ever pay off their debts. According to Jubilee USA Network, an organization advocating debt forgiveness in Africa, debt payments cost about 50 percent more than the loans were worth in the first place, forcing Africa to spend more money on these payments than on health care.

There is no doubt that forgiveness of the more than $300 billion debt could be helpful in creating the infrastructure necessary for Africa to succeed in the global economy. However, believing that no-strings-attached debt relief will alleviate poverty is like trying to cure cancer with a Band-Aid.

The greatest source of Africa's problems exists in its political leadership, not lack of aid from the G8 nations. Corrupt politicians line their own pockets with money designed to provide food, medicine and education to Africa's needy. The African Union estimated that corruption costs the continent $148 billion each year, enough money to wipe out the debt in just over two years.

Indeed, last month a report revealed that Nigeria's former rulers stole nearly $400 billion from the nation's treasury over a 40 year period. Dropping the debt and increasing aid to such regimes only serves to strengthen and embolden their abuses of power.

Other examples include Ugandan President Yoweri Museveni and Zimbabwean dictator Robert Mugabe. Dependent on foreign aid, Museveni is clinging to power. He recently amended the Ugandan Constitution to remove term limits, and many of his associates believe he wants to rule for life. Mugabe, also seeking aid, is one of Africa's most notorious dictators. Despite food shortages, he has excluded members from outside his political party from receiving U.N. aid and has destroyed the makeshift homes of thousands of the country's poorest citizens in an effort to "drive out the rubbish."

With corruption as Africa's greatest obstacle to development, democracy with private property rights and a free press would give the continent the best chance for redemption. Private property

---

> While surrounded by extreme poverty, [Botswana] has a sound economy and avoided the famine that devastated much of Africa in the 1980s.

---

rights give Africans a stake in improving their land and infrastructure and discourage environmental degradation while a free press works to hold the government accountable. According to Nobel Prize winning economist Amartya Sen, "no substantial famine has ever occurred in any independent and democratic country with a relatively free press."

Pockets of corruption will never completely disappear, and hard times come and go. Still, open, democratic governments have averted famine even in the midst of the most catastrophic disasters.

Take, for example, Botswana, one of Africa's rare democracies. While surrounded by extreme poverty, the country has a sound economy and avoided the famine that devastated much of Africa in the 1980s.

Botswana currently faces one of the worst AIDS epidemics in the world. However, between 1999 and 2003, the government increased AIDS funding from less than $5 million a year to more than $110 million. The money goes both for treatment and preventive measures, and Botswana's efforts may provide a model for other African nations to follow in decades to come. Meanwhile, Botswana's national debt makes up only 8.6 percent of its gross domestic product compared to 200 percent for neighboring Zimbabwe.

Why Democracies Don't Have Famines

By Miren Gutierrez
Inter Press Service, May 3, 2006

In Ethiopia, some 12.6 million people require food aid. Donors have pledged enough to meet about 82 percent of food needs, but only 54 percent has been delivered. Sound familiar? This alert was issued three years ago by the Famine Early Warning Systems Network, known as FEWS NET. But Ethiopia appeared again this year on FEWS NET's list of "current emergencies," alongside Somalia, Zimbabwe and Chad.

In a report on Ethiopia issued Feb. 24, the Food and Agriculture Organization (FAO) says that "about 15 million people are facing food insecurity that is either chronic or transitory in nature."

Of these, 5 million to 6 million are chronically food insecure (that is, "people who have lost the capacity to produce or buy enough to meet their annual food needs even under normal weather and market conditions"), and the remaining 10 million are vulnerable, "with a weak resilience to any shock," says FAO.

According to Oxfam International, a confederation of anti-poverty organizations, more than 850 million people suffer from chronic hunger. Is Ethiopia condemned to suffer hunger regularly? Are others?

"Abundance, not scarcity, best describes the world's food supply," said a 1998 paper entitled "12 Myths About Hunger," published by the Institute for Food and Development Policy/Food First, a U.S.-based non-governmental organization. "Even most 'hungry countries' have enough food for all their people right now. Many are net exporters of food and other agricultural products."

One could talk about the contradictions of hunger. For example, in Nigeria, Brazil or Bolivia, abundant food resources coexist with pockets of famine. Costa Rica has only half the number farmed hectares per person as Honduras, but Costa Ricans enjoy a life expectancy 11 years longer than that of Hondurans.

In Ethiopia, the 2005 harvest of cereal and pulse crops—which include peas and beans—was estimated by United Nations agencies FAO and the World Food Program (WFP) as "very good," and in 2006 the country has a small exportable surplus.

"Despite this positive overall situation, large numbers of people, mainly pastoralists in south-eastern Ethiopia, are facing pre-famine conditions due to the failure of seasonal rains," said a group of FAO experts in an e-mail interview.*

Similarly, another report published by FAO last December said that South Africa has harvested a record maize crop of 12.4 million tons. However, FAO added: "food insecurity in southern Africa is of serious concern. . . . Nearly 12 million people, mainly in Zimbabwe and Malawi, are in need of emergency food assistance."

According to FAO, the surplus of maize in the Republic of South Africa, at more than 4 million tons, is more than enough to meet the deficit of the rest of the countries in the region.

So why do people die of malnutrition and hunger?

The Malthusian nightmares of geometric population growth combined with an exhaustion of supplies have not materialized. The world's population has arrived at 6.4 billion, six times higher than when Thomas Malthus published his "Essay on the Principle of Pop-

---

Fighting displaces millions of people from their homes, leading to some of the world's worst hunger emergencies.—World Food Programme

---

ulation" in 1798. But Malthus had underestimated the human ability to exploit resources increasingly efficiently.

What humanity does not do so well is be fair with one another: most of the specialists and organizations dedicated to fighting against hunger, no matter how different their approach, point at inequality as the main underlying cause.

Amartya Sen, Nobel laureate in economics, argued that the lack of entitlement, rather than the lack of available food, is the principal cause of famine in poor countries.

According to Food First as well, famines are the result of "underlying inequities that deprive people, especially poor women, of economic opportunity and security. . . . Rapid population growth and hunger are endemic to societies where land ownership, jobs, education, health care, and old age security are beyond the reach of most people."

FAO says that "this is a question of unequal distribution, poverty and limited physical and economic access to food by large segments of the population."

Man-made disasters play an increasingly important role. According to WFP, "since 1992, the proportion of short- and long-term food crises that can be attributed to human causes has more than doubled, rising from 15 percent to more than 35 percent."

Fighting displaces millions of people from their homes, leading to some of the world's worst hunger emergencies, says WFP in a report available on its Web site. In war, food sometimes becomes a weapon:

soldiers will starve opponents by seizing food and livestock. Fields and water wells are often contaminated or destroyed in war, forcing farmers to abandon their land.

Famine is a complex process, not a unique, abrupt event. Food prices escalate, families sell their property, some of them migrate. As hunger grows, health systems collapse, the physical condition of individuals declines and people begin to die from malnutrition and illness, the report says.

Look at what is happening in Ethiopia. In spite of the advantages for crop-producing families, high cereal prices "will negatively affect the poorer households that are net buyers of grain," says FAO. As a consequence, "a significant number of vulnerable households remain largely food insecure and will depend on humanitarian assistance in 2006."

Asked about how the food crisis in the Horn of Africa compares with the situation in Zimbabwe, FAO replied that, "although this is not the only food crisis in Africa, it could be said that (the situation in the Horn of Africa) is currently the most dramatic due to the number of people affected and to their difficult food situation."

The crisis in Zimbabwe is more complicated, however. "Total cereal production has steadily fallen from over 3 million tons in 1996 to about 800,000 tons in 2005. This is a structural decline coinciding with the ongoing land tenure changes and the overall economic deterioration in that country."

President Robert Mugabe has given much of Zimbabwe's farmland to cronies not interested in farming; his policies have ruined the economy and left it short of diesel fuel to run its tractors. Inflation edged over 900 percent in March. The food crisis in southern Africa is occurring in the middle of the world's worst AIDS epidemic. Without sufficient food, those infected with HIV generally develop AIDS more rapidly and die.

"The greatest humanitarian crisis today is not in Pakistan, the tsunami region or Darfur, though they are all severe," said James Morris, executive director of WFP, last October. "It is the gradual disintegration of social structures in southern Africa."

The immediate cause of famine is widespread crop failure, resulting from drought or civil war. "But not every drought or crop failure has to lead to famine. Countries that are well prepared to handle the crisis manage to protect their vulnerable populations," says FAO.

The FAO experts reference Amartya Sen's work: "Democratic societies usually fare better in mitigating the food insecurity crisis and avoiding hardships to its population. One needs to highlight the importance of communication and the fact that often the risk of famine occurs because there is insufficient response to the early warning provided."

Sen put it like this in an article published by the British newspaper *The Observer* in 2002: "In democratic countries, even very poor ones, the survival of the ruling government would be threatened by famine, since elections are not easy to win after famines; nor is it easy to withstand criticism of opposition parties and newspapers. That is why famine does not occur in democratic countries."

Freedom Is Not Enough

By Joshua Hammer
Newsweek, November 14, 2005

Josiah Masiamphoka is tired of being a beggar. But the subsistence farmer and father of six lives in Malawi, where the rains have again failed to fall. The first time Masiamphoka was forced to take handouts was in 1994, when he lost most of his corn to drought. Then drought struck again in 1998, and again in 2002. Now the United Nations World Food Program has just announced a $150 million appeal to rescue Masiamphoka and millions of other people facing hunger and starvation in southern Africa. But WFP officials concede that a new appeal will likely be needed two or three years from now, when the rains fail again. "In the old days, people had food," says Masiamphoka, 59, whose family has subsisted for months on water lilies and shriveled sweet potatoes. "But it seems like God has decided to punish us."

How can the world rescue people like Masiamphoka from endless cycles of hunger and aid? Nobel Prize–winning Harvard economist Amartya Sen attracted worldwide attention in the 1980s when he offered an answer to the problem of starvation: more democracy. Sen contrasted the famines in repressive one-party states—Ethiopia in 1984 and China in the late 1950s and early 1960s—with successful efforts to manage food crises in nascent democracies such as Botswana. "Democracy gives the government a reason to prevent famine, because the penalty of famine is that the government can lose an election over it," says Sen. "A free press and public debate bring these issues into the forefront."

The theory makes perfect sense but has one problem: Malawi has had a multiparty system and a free press since 1994, when reformers ousted "Life President" Hastings Banda. Malawi rarely experienced a food crisis under the repressive Banda regime, which lasted 30 years; since Banda's demise, it's had several. "In 11 years we have gone backward, not forward," says Undule Mwakasungura, program director of Malawi's Centre for Human Rights and Rehabilitation. "We are poorer than we ever were."

Nobody is arguing from this that despotism is the solution. Banda murdered and tortured his political opponents. Per capita income reached only a little more than $200 a year during his reign, and child mortality was high. Moreover, Banda's policy of single-crop cultivation left a legacy of depleted soils and one of the worst crop-yield averages on earth. In the twilight of his rule, in 1993, the country did suffer a serious food shortage. But Malawians say he deserves credit for providing the country's 1 million subsistence farmers with subsidized seeds and fertilizer, and guaranteeing them world-market prices for their corn. "Banda was dictatorial, but at least he made sure that people never died of hunger," says Mwakasungura.

> Can massive aid be put to good use without capable leadership?

When Banda was ousted, international donors demanded that the new government lift budget-busting subsidies, taking away much of the farmers' safety net. Under the country's first elected president, Bakili Muluzi, corrupt officials fed on the spoils. In 2002 investigators discovered that parliamentarians and bureaucrats had looted the country's grain reserves and sold them at huge profits to international traders. The head of the Agricultural Development Marketing Corp. at the time, Friday Jumbe, allegedly earned more than $3 million from the sales, and poured $650,000 into the construction of a luxury hotel. The scandal hit just as the worst drought in a decade wiped out much of Malawi's harvest.

Malawi's democratic government has also done a poor job of managing the country's water. Despite a series of prolonged droughts, critics say, the Ministry of Agriculture and Irrigation has failed to exploit the country's two main water sources, the Shire River and Lake Malawi. Barely 1 percent of the country's arable land is irrigated, and peasant farmers remain almost entirely dependent on rainfall to survive. "We have wasted almost every drop of water we have," says Fidelis Mgowa, a rural-development expert with Catholic Relief Services in Blantyre. "Our democratic institutions are weak, and the government doesn't feel the pressure to do anything."

Sen argues that Malawi is the exception that proves the rule. He distinguishes between "functioning democracies" and "nonfunctioning democracies"—and puts Malawi firmly in the latter category. Other experts say that the problem in Malawi is not politics but poverty. Jeffrey Sachs, the noted economist and director of the Earth Institute at Columbia University, points out that since the Banda years, HIV has spread to nearly 20 percent of Malawi's population. Roads have deteriorated, the population has exploded (in spite of AIDS), the climate has worsened and chronic malnutrition has left a generation of stunted, damaged children.

Sachs says that throwing food relief at countries in dire need creates a culture of dependency. He believes that foreign donors need to invest $1 billion a year in Malawi over the next decade, or $70 per capita annually, in projects designed to get the population back on its feet. The money would go to seed, fertilizer, irrigation projects, road improvements, electrification, safe drinking water and health care. "The donors have been unwilling to face up to this," says Sachs. "They send food aid once people are dying, and it comes too late and too little. But they don't help the country grow the food."

But can massive aid be put to good use without capable leadership? Malawi's current president, Bingu wa Mutharika, is a former U.N. trade expert who earned a master's degree in economics in the United States. He has promised to clean up corruption and has made agricultural development a priority. But Mutharika has been embroiled in a dispute with opponents that has all but paralyzed his government. Last month, rivals, led by former president Muluzi, launched impeachment proceedings against him, claiming that he had misused public funds. Mutharika claims that he is the victim of a campaign by crooked politicians who fear being caught up in his anticorruption drive. In rural areas, some peasant farmers have reacted to the impeachment effort with disgust. "As soon as these politicians are elected, that's the end of it," says Josiah Masiamphoka, walking past parched fields sprawling just a few hundred yards from the Shire River. "They have nothing to do with the people who put them in power." Masiamphoka wouldn't have dared make such a statement under Hastings Banda. But then, he also had food on his table.

II. FAMINES IN THE WORLD TODAY

Editor's Introduction

Famines throughout world history have run in cycles, occurring in different parts of the globe at different times, from northwestern England in the 1620s, to the Great Famine of Ireland in 1847, to China in the early 1960s, and to Bangladesh in the 1970s, to name but a few. Today, the vast majority of famine occurs in Africa, specifically sub-Saharan Africa, the region of the continent south of the Sahara Desert. Sub-Saharan Africa's chronic poverty, considered the worst in the world, is exacerbated by natural disasters, political corruption, and armed conflicts. This chapter explores the causes and effects of famine in four African nations, as well as in North Korea, the nation with the most severe hunger crisis outside of Africa.

One of the countries most recently affected by famine is Niger, where hunger is not directly tied to conspicuous causes such as war, natural disasters, or political corruption. Those kinds of famines generate press coverage, which in turn generates aid, even if it is not enough. The famine in Niger, as Samuel Loewenberg explains in "Millions in Niger Facing Food Shortages Once Again," is a product of chronic poverty, a distinctly less newsworthy condition. Since it receives less attention than other food crises, the situation in Niger is even more desperate, inspiring one tribe to create a new phrase, "Dabary ban," which Loewenberg translates as "all hope is lost, there is nothing left to do."

Poor weather conditions are increasingly destabilizing Kenya's food supply, an author for *The Nation* reports in "Season of Many Hungers." The people of Kenya suffered droughts from 1992 to 1993, 1996 to 1997, and 1998 to 2001, as well as floods from 1997 to 2001. Though Kenya's situation is frequently described as chronic food insecurity, rather than famine, it is considered particularly vulnerable to famine, especially as global climate change accelerates and further restricts farmers' ability to plant crops and graze livestock.

In Malawi, international politics has severely worsened a pre-existing hunger crisis. In "Who Caused the Malawi Famine?" Kwesi Owusu and Francis Ng'ambi investigate the series of events precipitating the starvation of almost 70 percent of the nation's farming families. Acting under advice from the International Monetary Fund (IMF), Malawi had sold a large amount of its strategic grain reserves. When famine came, the country no longer had its emergency stockpiles. At the same time, corruption within the Malawi government led many donor nations as well as the IMF to withdraw aid, making it even more difficult for the country to address its debilitating famine.

Political corruption is the main obstacle for citizens trying to obtain food in Zimbabwe, Gabrielle Menezes writes in "Letter from Zimbabwe." With the government in control of the majority of food aid, the ruling party can easily trade food for votes. "To give food aid in a politicized environment is compli-cated," Menezes writes; "it is the ultimate political weapon, and something the government needs to control at all costs to maintain its position."

The final article in this chapter leaves sub-Saharan Africa for North Korea, where famine is a direct effect of not only political corruption, but also political repression. In "Glimpses of a Hermit Nation: Trading Ideals for Sustenance," Barbara Demick reports that North Korea's chronic hunger—and the accom-panying deaths of its citizens from starvation—is one of the main factors influ-encing political disillusionment and defection in the totalitarian state.

Millions in Niger Facing Food Shortages Once Again

BY SAMUEL LOEWENBERG
THE LANCET, MAY 6, 2006

In a rudimentary medical clinic on the southern edge of the Sahara desert, a baby is taken from his mother's arms. He is placed inside a black harness attached to handheld scale. All of his ribs are visible, his limbs are emaciated. The child is 10 months old. He weighs 4 kg, down from 5 kg 2 months earlier. He should weigh twice as much.

By the harsh calculations of the feeding centre, one could say the child is lucky. He is so badly underweight he will receive a ration of therapeutic feeding: 3.5 g of enriched cornmeal and oil. Resources are so badly stretched here that out of the 200 children brought here by their mothers, only a third will receive food.

"People get upset, but we only have enough supplies to help a few of them," says Ibrahim Chalaré, the field coordinator for the feeding centre, which is run by the British charity Islamic Relief. Childhood hunger is a perennial problem in this landlocked sub-Saharan country, but it is unusual to see so many malnourished children so early in the year, he says. Rates of admission are double what they were last month, Chalaré continues, and he expects it to triple by summer.

More than 2 million people in this West African country are facing acute malnutrition. Most of them are children.

Normally at this time of the year the villagers still have plenty of food left over from the harvest season. In fact, the rains were good this past year, and the harvest was bountiful. But the food shortages of last summer left many people weakened and indebted, and they have already exhausted their supplies.

A few hours to the south, in the capital city of Niamey, the outdoor markets overflow with fresh meat and vegetables. But Niger is one of the poorest nations in the world, and even in good times that bounty is beyond the reach of most of the country's rural population.

In the vicious cycle of sub-Saharan nations in chronic poverty, any disruption can quickly throw millions into a hunger crisis. Once a food shortage hits, grain prices skyrocket, as they did last year.

Even with the bountiful harvest this year, grain prices are already twice the normal price in many districts, leaving them out of reach of millions of rural Nigeriens.

In a therapeutic feeding clinic for severely malnourished children, Foure Souley rests her 2-year-old child on her lap. The child's body is so wasted, at only 4.5 kg, that she cannot support the weight of her own head. She looks like a broken doll.

When Mrs Souley is asked what she will do when she leaves the feeding centre after her child is released in a few weeks, she shrugs and says "Dabary ban." It is a new phrase in her tribe's language that has come into use since the recent hunger crises. It means that all hope is lost, there is nothing left to do.

Unlike the more high-profile food crises in Ethiopia and Sudan, the malnutrition problem here is not due to the armed conflict, natural disaster, or corruption. Simply put, the problem is chronic poverty. Malnutrition rates throughout this sub-Saharan region have exceeded the World Health Organization's crisis threshold for more than a decade.

> In the vicious cycle of sub-Saharan nations in chronic poverty, any disruption can quickly throw millions into a hunger crisis.

"Niger is such a poor country that we've gotten used to the idea that one in five children die before the age of five," says Jeremy Lester, the European Union's chief of mission for Niger. An October, 2005 study by UNICEF found that 15.3% of Niger's 6 to 59 month old children suffer from severe or moderate malnutrition.

The international community does seem to be slowly waking up to the problem of chronic hunger. Unlike last year, when the World Food Programme's pleas for emergency assistance were virtually ignored until famine conditions had set in, this year the USA and the EU have already funded half of the WFP's US$25 million aid request.

But even with these commitments, thousands are already suffering and the feeding centres are jammed. The current crisis is an example of how the wealthy countries that fund relief efforts so often miss the most crucial moment: the months before hunger becomes widespread.

"Children are already falling into acute malnutrition. The aid money and food will arrive too late," says Johannes Sekenes, a Norwegian nurse who has headed up the Médecins Sans Frontières (MSF) operation here since 2004. She says that the MSF therapeutic feeding operation last year was the largest in her organisation's history. A striking fact, since MSF usually operates in war zones and disaster areas.

The Politics of Food Aid

As with most things in the twisted world of international famine relief, the term "food aid" itself is duplicitous. The USA, for instance, gives by far the most food aid of any country. But that's not quite what it seems. While most of the world gives aid agencies cash which they use to buy food locally, 99% of the food aid provided by the USA is purchased from American farmers at market prices and is then shipped overseas on US registered vessels (the vast majority of container ships are registered in countries like Liberia and Panama; the US registered container ships used in the feeding programme are almost an anachronism, kept alive in part because of this aid programme).

By general consensus, US food aid is inefficient, overpriced, and can be damaging to the African economy. The *Financial Times* called the American type of assistance "a subsidy programme for rich world farmers," such as American agro-giants Cargill and Archer-Daniels Midland. According to the Paris-based Organisation for Economic Cooperation and Development, this kind of direct food aid can take 5 months or more to arrive and costs 50% more than if the assistance had been given as cash used to buy food locally. Also, it tends to undercut local markets. If the assistance had been provided as cash, it would have added US$750 million to the approximately $4 billion in food aid already donated by rich countries.

Under increasing pressure to reform its food-only aid approach, last year the Bush Administration tried to get Congress to pass legislation allowing for one quarter of American emergency assistance to be delivered in cash instead of as processed crop purchases. Administration aid officials argued that the USA would be able to provide twice as much food for the same money because of the savings on transportation alone.

But even with the Bush Administration behind it, the proposal went nowhere. It was killed by agro-business, the shipping industry, and the farm-state congressmen that control food aid. Ironically, they had lobbying assistance not only from agro-business giants and shipping companies, but also from charity aid agencies such as Catholic Relief Services and Care. Why? Because the aid agencies sell much of the food they receive to pay for other programmes such as health care and development assistance that they provide to impoverished nations.

Despite the EU's supposed interest in long-term development, only a small percentage of the money it gives to Niger is directed towards sustainable agricultural projects like directed donations of fertiliser and high-potency seed. The USA, the world's largest donor, spent $1.4 billion in emergency aid in Africa last year, but only one tenth that much in long-term development. "The system of foreign aid is very political. Does it makes sense? No," says Andrew Natsios, the former chief of overseas assistance in the Bush Administration.

For Niger, with its paucity of resources, hunger is only one of a plethora of public-health problems that range from tropical diseases to single-digit rates of literacy. Niger sits at the bottom of the United Nation's Human Development Index, which assesses factors like poverty, education, and life expectancy.

Delivering Health Care in Niger

Alassane Seydou is used to working in conditions that many physicians would find intolerable. The young doctor does not practice in a desert field station. He is a specialist in internal medicine and rheumatology at the National Hospital of Niamey.

It is hard to imagine a medical centre in a capital city that is more strapped for resources. Basics like saline solution and adrenaline are in short supply. In the malnutrition and malaria wards, which consist of little more than beds jammed into a room, flies land on the infant patients.

Outside the infants' ward there is a small garden. Chickens walk amongst the flowers, a stark reminder that Niger is ill equipped to deal with its recent spate of avian influenza. The 850-bed hospital is not free. Patients must pay, no matter how poor. Resources are so sparse here that families must provide their own food, even in the malnourished ward.

This is the only major hospital in Niger, and patients come from all over the country as we from the neighbouring nations of Burkina Faso and Nigeria. The most widespread ailments are AIDS, malaria, and tuberculosis, says Seydou. Around 10% of their patients also suffer from acute malnutrition. One of the biggest frustrations, says Seydou, is that lack the resources for basic preventive care. Liver cancer due to hepatitis B is one of the most common illnesses he has to treat. The neighbouring countries of Burkina Faso and Benin have programmes for childhood hepatitis vaccinations, but these are out of reach in Niger, a nation that is the poorest of the poor in sub-Saharan Africa. As Seydou roams the hospital grounds, where families are camped out among the buildings waiting for their relatives to heal, he is approached by a woman begging for money. There is nothing he can do for her.

Basic access to health care is out of reach for the vast majority of the population. Some villages have rudimentary clinics, often little more than dispensaries of the most basic medicines. Souley, like all of the mothers at the feeding centre, walked hours along desert roads to bring her child to the feeding centre.

Another of the crucial problems that must be addressed, say public health advocates, is the issue of education, especially for women. Literacy rates in Niger are among the lowest in the world. More than half of the Nigerien girls have no schooling, and overall only 9.4% of women are literate.

"If girls go to school, they will have less children, better jobs, and less disease," says Carol Añonuevo, a senior researcher at the UNESCO Institute of Education who is conducting a study of sub-Saharan Africa.

There is no simple fix to any of these problems. Many development experts note that Africa has received billions of dollars in aid during the past 50 years, but has little to show for it.

The new trend seems to be directed towards programmes that treat specific symptoms of poverty, rather than vast grants of dollars to ineffectual governments. In one example, the Red Cross gave small cash grants to 5000 households in 88 villages. The results were promising, says the Red Cross' Emmanuelle Osmond. The women, to whom the money was given, used it to buy food, pay off debts, and buy livestock and clothes. In one village, the women pooled their money to buy a donkey cart they could use as an ambulance to get to the health centre in the next village.

At the macro level, many development specialists say that the only way to break the cycle of hunger is to provide agricultural assistance so Nigeriens can feed themselves. Africa has never received the kind of long-term agricultural development assistance—such as fertiliser and high-yield seeds—that successfully helped reduce hunger in Asia and Latin America in the 1960s and 1970s, said Peter Timmer, a former development economist at Harvard University. "Neither the donors nor the countries themselves have tried that kind of massive investment in rural economies," he says.

Season of Many Hungers

THE NATION, DECEMBER 19, 2005

Robert Rose rolls a pen between his fingers, then raises his head and asks: "Famine? There has not been famine in Kenya. There has been mitigation."

A programme officer with the World Food Programme (WFP), Rose, while trying to demystify a "general misconception," explains that what has often been reported as famine in parts of the country is, in fact, persistent food insecurity or chronic hunger.

"It becomes a famine when there are mass deaths arising from a complete absence of food," he says.

Away from terminology issues, discussions with Rose, officials of Famine Early Warning Systems Network (Fews-Net) and the Government's Arid Lands Resource Management Project (ALRMP), all of whom are members of the Kenya Food Security Steering Group (KFSSG), point towards improper land use by communities, changing climatic conditions, and lacklustre performance by authorities in the affected regions.

Latest information reveal that food insecurity in 17 districts across the country is alarming, and could get worse as the year turns.

The short rains, on which the affected lowlands depend for food production, are failing, says Nancy Mutunga of Fews-Net and James Oduor of ALRMP.

This is after repeated seasons of bad weather. In pastoralist areas, for example, even the hardy camels are reportedly dying of extreme weather conditions. Droughts and floods have chronologically replaced each other in some regions.

Both Oduor and Mutunga say the frequency of poor weather conditions is becoming more regular and unusually prolonged. This has particularly been observed within the past 10 years. Increasing frequency and duration of drought, in particular, have destabilised coping strategies of affected communities. Many have been stretched beyond survival limits.

"This is visible in increasing levels of destitution and a rising number of pastoralist drop-outs, for example, appearing in urban centres," says Mutunga. She says it is a result of reduced pasture and declining numbers of livestock, forcing patoralists out of their traditional ways.

Besides climatic reasons, it is now noted that a major contributor to perennial hunger in the 17 affected districts is linked to rigid practices and incapability among locals, and sometimes negligence by authorities.

In order of severity, the arid areas of Baringo, Turkana and Samburu in the North Rift region, Isiolo, Marsabit, Makueni and Moyale in Eastern, the whole of North Eastern Province, and Tana River in Coast Province, top the list.

Extreme weather patterns, marked by a prolonged absence of rain and, sometimes, floods combine with poor development indicators and stiff lifestyles to make people here highly vulnerable.

Most inhabitants of these areas, being pastoralists, derive their livelihood entirely from livestock. This has played against them lately. When drought strikes, animals die for lack of pasture and

---

Besides climatic reasons, it is now noted that a major contributor to perennial hunger . . . is linked to rigid practices and incapability among locals, and sometimes negligence by authorities.

---

water. The immediate sufferers are children. They become malnourished as milk, their only source of proper nutrition, diminishes.

These areas also have poor indicators of development. Education levels are low and infrastructure is poor. "Pastoralists rely on markets, yet these areas lack proper structures and roads," says Oduor.

The long distances that people trek to the markets are serious setbacks and worsen when animals are weakened by harsh weather. Add these to general insecurity, poor health and widespread poverty, among other unfavourable factors.

Yet this is what the people have endured for the past 10 years—bad weather. Droughts in 1992–93, 1996–97 and 1998–2001, floods in 1997 to 2001, and the current agro-climatic changes have only heightened food insecurity in these regions.

There has been a consistent reduction of livestock productivity owing to "inadequate availability of key fundamentals—water, pasture and browse," according to information from Fews-Net. This has led to many deaths in the area.

Hardship coping mechanisms have also been eroded. Mutunga, the Kenya representative for Fews-Net, says pastoralists had ways of withstanding the extremities of weather, but these have now been interrupted by prolonged climatic changes and increased encroachment on reserve land.

"There used to be designated areas for grazing during wet and dry seasons. During wet seasons, pastoralists grazed their animals around their homesteads. They moved to special areas further away only when the dry season set in. Now there are no dry season areas," she says.

This is not only because of sustained poor weather but also encroachment by people for settlement and charcoal burning practices. Worse, these communities are unable to "develop and adopt new productive initiatives."

Rose cites education as the key, saying it would enhance the people's ability to develop quick escape alternatives. Livestock are not easily recoverable assets, adds Mutunga.

Currently, livestock prices have fallen drastically in some areas, accentuating poverty levels. A few months ago, a resident of Kitui, for example, lamented the declining prices of goats in the area, saying he had sold one for about Sh300.

In marginal agricultural areas, mostly the lowlands of Eastern Province, such as Ukambani, a sustained population pressure has pushed people from the comparatively more productive highland to the unproductive lower sections.

As they shift, the communities practise the same agricultural methods of the higher grounds, which is mainly production of maize. The result has been mass failure of the crop. Parts of Makueni district, for example, are affected, particularly the southern divisions of Kathonzweni, Makindu, Kibwezi, and Mtito Andei.

A drive around Kathonzweni division reveals crop failure in households that planted maize at the start of the last season a month ago. The ones who went for crops like cassava and cowpeas may have a harvest, at least in the first quarter of next year.

"One of the key problems in marginal agricultural areas is enterprise. Some households have moved from the highlands and transferred their planting habits to the lower zones," says Mutunga. "They try to grow maize as they did on the higher ground, but this is not the right crop for some of these places. The result is persistent crop failure," adds Rose.

The lower areas, he points out, are more conducive to production of hardy crops like cassava, millet and sorghum, but which the present generation is uninterested in.

"A change of attitude is needed here," says Mutunga. This compounds the communities' state of unpreparedness when rains fail, and is exactly what has happened. "The failed 2005 long rains represent the second consecutive poor season," says last month's Kenya Food Security Update, jointly produced by the Government, Fews-Net and WFP.

The document says poor start of the critical short rains has raised fears of a worsening situation. The season contributes close to 70 per cent of farm output in the lowlands of Makueni, Kitui, Malindi, Kwale, Kilifi and Taita Taveta districts. Catastrophic food insecurity cannot be ruled out.

The current emergency intervention, planned to end in February 2006, may be extended, Oduor says. "If rains fail, as they are likely to, we shall start another emergency intervention from March to August 2006."

For instance, six divisions in Makueni—namely Kibwezi, Mtito Andei, Nguu, Kathonzweni, Kalawa and Makindu—are listed by the district's drought monitoring team, headed by Daniel Mbuvi, as experiencing a worsening scenario.

Experts are beginning to note a marked rise in stunted children in these areas, suggesting an unresolved problem.

"The nutritional status of children under five years is deteriorating," says Mbuvi. Frustrated farmers are now intensifying charcoal burning and sand harvesting as coping strategies.

Authorities are beginning to express fear that the level at which these activities are being conducted will be disastrous to the environment. Charcoal sacks marked for sale dot the dusty road linking Wote (Makueni's main town) and Makindu, selling at Sh200.

Undeniably, food insecurity in most of the marginal agricultural regions date back to the late nineties, when a dangerous swing of weather between floods and drought hit the country.

According to Oduor, the first of a series of interventions started after the drought of 1999 to 2000. Between May 2000 and September 2002, 26 districts across the country received emergency assistance valued at about 360 million US dollars. About 3.3 million people needed this relief.

There was then a temporary reprieve until September 2004, when it again emerged that about 2.6 million people were in need of aid. This was supplied at a price of 100 million US dollars, until February this year. Again, 26 districts were affected.

Emergency food requirement has been persistent since then. Between March and August this year, about 60 million US dollars has been spent to support over two million food-insecure people in 21 districts. The on-going phase of assistance is to cater for 1.2 starving people in 17 districts. By February next year, about 32.5 million US dollars will have been spent.

Going by a recent observation in Makueni and the reports generated from there and other agro-ecological zones, Oduor's fear that emergency food assistance may go beyond February next year may be well founded.

These emergency operations, known among humanitarian personnel as EMOP, are the mitigation Rose refers to. They have prevented a possible outbreak of famine.

Who Caused the Malawi Famine?

BY KWESI OWUSU AND FRANCIS NG'AMBI
AFRICAN BUSINESS, JANUARY 2003

During May 2002, following warnings by UN agencies of a food crisis affecting approximately 13m people in Southern Africa, Malawi hit the world media headlines with reports of widespread deaths from hunger and hunger related diseases. The estimates varied from 500 to several thousand, making the current food crisis worse than the fabled Nyasaland famine of 1949. At the height of the current crisis, nearly 70% of farming families were without food and starving, up from 31% during the same period last year.

When the authors of this report visited villages near Salima in the Central region in August 2002, food stocks and emergency aid supplies were depleted and the impoverished communities faced starvation. Many families were desperate for food and had resorted to eating maize husks and wild potatoes. We saw several freshly dug graves, indicating that far from tailing off, the death toll from hunger was still mounting in these remote parts of Malawi.

The food crisis coincided in April 2002 with Malawi's suspension from Highly Indebted Poor Country (HIPC) interim debt relief by the International Monetary Fund (IMF) and the World Bank, and subsequent controversy over corruption allegations against the Malawi Government and the fatal mismanagement of the country's strategic grain reserves. These events left the country tragically short of food and triggered a national crisis.

The decision to sell Malawi's grain reserves followed advice from the IMF to reduce operational costs and the level of buffer stocks held from 167,000 tons to 60,000 tons, in order to repay a South African bank for a commercial loan of $300m, incurred by the National Food Reserve Agency (NFRA) when it was established as a quasi-independent agency.

The IMF further advised that the maize be exported to neighbouring countries, in disregard of the impending food crisis in Malawi. In the event, and evidently in clear defiance of the IMF, the Malawi Government sold almost all of the 167,000 tons reserve, much of it on local markets, to private traders, the new agents of the partially liberalised grain market. Traders stockpiled it and later profiteered from hunger.

Since then, all parties to the gross mismanagement of the country's food security policy have traded accusations and refused to take responsibility for their failures.

The IMF categorically disowned its advice to the Malawi Government, stating they had "no expertise in food security policy and we did not instruct the Malawi Government or the National Food Reserve Agency (NFRA) to dispose of the reserves."

Horst Kohler, the IMF Managing Director, repeated the denial when he appeared before a British Parliamentary Committee on July 4, 2002, but came close to admitting responsibility under questioning: "I want to underline: this is an issue in the responsibility of the World Bank and the EU Commission. The IMF was part of this process of giving advice to the Malawi Government and the IMF may also have not been attentive enough, but I just tell you that I am not accepting that the IMF is made the culprit for this case and I really also will go public if it continues, this kind of accusation. I have sent the President of Malawi a letter in which I made clear that he was involved with the World Bank and the EU Commission in this project; that the IMF was part of, say, the kind of international advice and the IMF may, again, not have been attentive enough how they exercised how to run this maize stock, but it was not the responsibility of the Fund to implement the advice. It is clearly an issue to think how we can avoid that this kind of mistake will happen again."

At a meeting of the Malawi NGOs and the World Bank Consultative Group in Lilongwe on August 6, 2002, Dunstan Wai, the new World Bank Director for Malawi, spoke candidly about the grain sale, but added another twist to the story by claiming that much of the stored grain was "rotten" and needed to be sold.

Which prompts further concerns: whether the IMF, the World Bank, and the European Commission, individually or collectively acted legally when they advised Malawi to sell "rotten" and possibly unsafe food to the public. The Malawi Government, in turn, denied all responsibility and delayed declaring an emergency until late February 2002, when civil society organisations and the media presented irrefutable evidence of hunger related deaths. However, by June 2002 President Muluzi had not only accepted that there was a crisis, but said, "the IMF is to blame for the biting food crisis . . . they insisted the government sell maize from its strategic reserve and requested that the government abandon its starter pack agricultural subsidy program."

The rapidly deteriorating relationship between the Malawi and its foreign financiers go back to July 2000 when a Parliamentary Public Accounts Committee published a highly critical report on corruption and fraud within the government.

In October 2000, for instance, the British High Commissioner rebuked the Malawi government for being soft on corruption and threatened to withdraw aid. The dispute escalated and reached a critical point in November 2001 when several major donors, including the UK, EU, Denmark and the US suspended their aid programmes. The Malawi government took this badly, at a time when it needed to import food to off set the worsening food shortages.

The diplomatic crisis continued and reached another critical point in 2002, when the donors raised suspicions about some Government officials profiteering from the emptying of the Strategic Grain Reserve (SGR) silos. By May 2002, the IMF delayed the disbursement of $47m in loans to Malawi because it had overspent its budget by $45m (1.9% of GDP).

Malawi was also suspended from interim debt relief under HIPC, thereby adding $4m more to annual debt payments. Other donors took their cue from the IMF and froze development aid to Malawi.

> The [Malawi] famine claimed more victims, mostly the very poor and socially marginalised, particularly in the remote and inaccessible parts of the country.

However, many Malawians, while acutely aware of the need to combat corruption and strengthen governance, still accuse the donors of using the corruption issue to penalise the government for defying their instructions not to sell the reserve grain on the local market. Corruption is also used as a lever to impose donor conditionality and to penalise Malawi for not meeting certain macro-economic targets and for delays in privatisation, at least partly due to public opposition.

The sale of grain controversy and donor relief led to the international humanitarian relief grinding to a halt, having barely started. The food aid that trickled in was poorly distributed or found its way onto the market, including most of the 11,860 tons of maize from the European Commission.

The famine claimed more victims, mostly the very poor and socially marginalised, particularly in the remote and inaccessible parts of the country. The Anti-Corruption Bureau, a donor-funded body, recently strengthened to investigate high corruption cases, published its findings into the sale of grain by the Strategic Grain Reserve Agency (SGRA).

It found no specific acts of corruption but reprimanded two senior members in Muluzi's government for "criminal recklessness and negligence." One was dropped from the Cabinet and together with three managers of the Strategic Grain Reserve Agency, is awaiting legal prosecution.

The Catholic Commission for Peace released a list of names of purchasers of SGR maize, which included a number of prominent people who, "knew about the coming food price hike, so they bought grain from the SGR and withdrew these stocks from the market, driving prices up and creating an artificial shortage."

The Malawi Government ordered an internal audit of the NFRA, which was published in June 2002. But as the Civil Society Agricultural Network (CISANET) commented, "stakeholders would need access to a detailed report to come to a full judgement on the issues raised and the quality and depth of the audit process." Crucially, the audit does not cover the post-2002 period for which most concerns have been raised.

Pressure is also mounting within Malawi for a fitting apology to the families of the famine victims.

The lack of publicly available information remains a key issue. The donors have criticised the Malawi Government for a lack of transparency, but have themselves refused to publish key documents, including the European Commission's report that was used by the IMF as a basis for its advice on grain stocks. Other important documents, such as the schedule for privatisation of the Agriculture Development and Marketing Corporation (ADMARC), have recently been released but have not included any consultation with civil society or Parliamentarians. The lack of public transparency in donor advice and conditionality undermines the efforts of civil society in Malawi to hold their government to account.

Letter from Zimbabwe

By Gabrielle Menezes
The Nation, May 12, 2003

The ravages of drought are evident to anyone traveling through Zimbabwe. The carcass of a dead donkey lies on the road, while skeletal dogs tear at its intestines. The majestic Save River, once deep enough for hippos to wallow in, can now be crossed by foot. Government estates, however, are green with winter wheat and maize, irrigated by reservoir water. In contrast, privately owned commercial farms, which should have provided about a third of Zimbabwe's maize, have melted into the surrounding dry bush. Food aid from abroad must now make up for these lost harvests.

Famine anywhere is a tragedy, but when it is caused by a country's government it is an unspeakable crime. This is what makes the starving millions in Zimbabwe different from those in other Southern African countries enduring famine. Zimbabwe used to be the breadbasket of the region. President Robert Mugabe's chaotic land-reform policies and the widespread illegal farm invasions he encouraged make the government partly responsible for the famine, which it is now exploiting for its own survival. To give food aid in a politicized environment is complicated; it is the ultimate political weapon, and something the government needs to control at all costs to maintain its position.

Mealie-meal is the staple food of Zimbabwe. A white powder made from ground maize, it is used to make a thick porridge called *sadza*. Maize is becoming increasingly rare. In the capital, Harare, a seething mass of people queuing for maize can easily be mistaken for a riot. The main way of getting mealie-meal in Zimbabwe is through the government-controlled Grain Marketing Board, where maize can be bought at controlled prices. The government, conveniently, has kept a monopoly on importing maize, and very few import licenses have been granted to nongovernmental organizations. Anyone who supports the political opposition, the Movement for Democratic Change (MDC), or anyone who does not support Mugabe's ruling party, the Zimbabwe African National Union–Patriotic Front (ZANU-PF), is not sold food.

Felix (who doesn't want to use his last name for fear of retribution) is typical of people who have been unable to get mealie-meal because they don't have party cards. Although he works as a gardener in one of Harare's affluent suburbs and earns above the average wage, Felix's children recently went for three days without food. "You know, to get mealie-meal in Zimbabwe it is now very tough," Felix says. "To get it you first have to get a ZANU-PF card. But even at the Grain Marketing Board, people are not getting maize, so people are dying of hunger."

The second way of getting food is by registering in a government "food for work" program. Traditionally, in times of drought, families with no harvest and no money to purchase food perform public labor—for example, repairing rural roads—in return for food. In many instances MDC supporters have not been allowed to register for food-for-work programs.

There is also a third way of getting food, which is from international food aid programs. The largest such program is the United Nations World Food Program, which contracts with local organizations to distribute its food aid. The catch is that NGOs used by the WFP need to be registered by the Zimbabwean government.

When asked, most of the children say they eat just one meal of sadza a day.

Christian Care, one of the NGOs that give out WFP food, reluctantly agreed to let me travel with them to food distribution points. Courage Chirove, a refreshingly down-to-earth aid worker, drives me to the village of Rimai. Hidden among bushes and trees, it is miles away from a paved road, not to mention a town. When we arrive, people are patiently waiting for food to be distributed. Some of the women have walked four miles; they will walk back the same way, gracefully balancing kilos of maize and beans on their heads, and with children tied around their waists. The signs of malnutrition are beginning to be visible in the children in the waiting crowd. Their bellies beneath ragged T-shirts are slightly distended; their twiglike arms are shrinking to bone. Their eyes are large in their faces. When asked, most of the children say they eat just one meal of *sadza* a day.

Food in Rimai is kept in the schoolhouse, the only concrete building in the area big enough to store the hundreds of WFP maize bags. There's not enough food for everyone, so there are registers of those most in need: orphans, widows, pregnant women and child-headed households. The WFP believes it is important to involve the community in giving out food aid, so the registers are compiled by community leaders. However, in such a politicized environment as Zimbabwe, this may not be such a good idea. Community leaders with political affiliations are able to manipulate the registers. This is likely to happen in places like Rimai, where many villagers support the opposition but where ZANU-PF officials are in charge.

The headmaster of Rimai is a community leader. A slight man with an unctuous smile, he welcomes me into his office. Behind him is a ZANU-PF poster for the 2002 elections, showing how to vote by neatly ticking the box that says ZANU-PF. On another wall a framed portrait of Mugabe takes pride of place. Posters like these are not supposed to be around any of the food distribution points. As one WFP worker told me, there are many ways to intimidate people.

It is hard to ask questions in Zimbabwe. People are afraid to answer and are suspicious of those who ask them. The headmaster follows me around as I try to talk to people. He assures me that all the food distribution has been fair. Later, however, a Christian Care worker admits to me that there have been political problems with the registers. She hastens to add that now the registers are in order. Maybe.

"In Rimai," says Chirove, "there are war veterans on the committee. The government uses war veterans badly, but we have only had a problem with the ones who are partisan." The people who fought in Zimbabwe's liberation war have traditionally been supporters of Mugabe and his ZANU-PF party. In 1997 the veterans, incensed at the wealth that politicians had amassed for themselves while they remained in poverty, demanded money and later land. The government acquiesced in their wishes, and began its chaotic land-reform program. The war vets have since been seen as instruments of Mugabe's policies to cleanse the land of white farmers.

While I am in Rimai, Chirove goes to a village meeting to get people to revise their registers. After he picks me up, and once we are in the privacy of the car, he tells me that war veterans and the CIO (the Central Intelligence Organization, Zimbabwe's feared secret police) invited themselves along to the meeting. The war vets and CIO claimed that Christian Care is acting as an agent of the opposition. They said that posters with the MDC logo, an open hand, were found in the bags of maize being distributed. This allegation is pure fiction. All the blue-and-white WFP bags are sealed. "That this is not government food had incensed people," says Chirove. "The war vets said to withdraw the statement by one of the staff that the food aid had nothing to do with the government, and that Christian Care should not tamper with the registers. The police said some of the statements might lead to violence." Chirove says he eventually managed to placate the war vets, telling them, "The WFP is a branch of the UN. Zimbabwe is a member of the UN, and that's why we're getting help."

Weeks later, Christian Care admits to me that one of its program administrators was kidnapped by war veterans and held overnight, but quickly insists that it has had no further problems with the vets. Although problems are meant to be reported to the WFP, one WFP worker is surprised when I tell her about the efforts to intimidate Christian Care personnel.

Christian Care is not the only NGO that has been experiencing problems distributing aid. Care International in the Chivi District and in Mberengwa East have received complaints that their registers favor supporters of Mugabe's regime. Although NGOs have shown a willingness to intervene when problems arise, human rights organizations say that generally problems are not reported.

The World Food Program is in a difficult position. It has to be invited into a country and work with that country's government. Like all UN organizations, it bends over backward to be seen as impartial. The situation in Zimbabwe once again raises the issue of whether this policy of impartiality can fairly be seen as going along with government policy, which in this case is discriminatory. Some organizations, like the Catholic Commission, suspended their feeding programs, refusing to allow war vets or the government to tell them whom they can or can't feed. But for a humanitarian organization to withdraw aid is especially repugnant. In Chirove's opinion, "If you withdraw aid, the person who caused the problem doesn't suffer."

Back in Rimai, food distribution goes on all day. Women energetically check registers and weigh food under the parching sun. Some WFP bags of food are missing, and a group of leaders argue about what to do. Who should be given less food? In the middle of this debate a man taps me discreetly on the shoulder. "Sister, you are wanted," he says. I follow him into an empty classroom where I am presented with a plate of food and a miraculous glass of water. On the plate is a mound of sadza and some dubious meat. This is more food that most of the people here will eat in two days. But a guest is sacred, and according to the dictates of hospitality starving people must now feed me. In this country tormented by famine, twisted politics and violence, I have been given a glimpse of something else.

Glimpses of a Hermit Nation

Trading Ideals for Sustenance

By Barbara Demick
Los Angeles Times, July 4, 2005

For most of her life, Kim Hui Suk had spouted the sayings of North Korea's founder Kim Il Sung and never for a moment harbored a doubt: Capitalists were the enemy. Individualism was evil.

But then disaster rained down on her hometown, Chongjin, on North Korea's remote east coast. Factories ran out of fuel. Food rations stopped. Watching her family slowly succumb to the famine—her mother-in-law, husband and son eventually would die of starvation—Kim realized she had to change.

Once a stickler for following the rules, she bribed a bureaucrat so she could sell her apartment. Then, with no business skills other than the ability to calculate on an abacus, she used the proceeds of the sale to set herself up in a black market business, hawking biscuits and moonshine she brewed from corn.

Kim could have been sent away for life for such crimes. But obeying the rules would have meant a death sentence.

"The simple and kind-hearted people who did what they were told—they were the first to die of starvation," said Kim, a soft-spoken grandmother who now lives in South Korea and has adopted a new name to protect family members still in the North.

The famine that killed 2 million North Koreans in the mid-1990s and the death of the nation's founder, Kim Il Sung, in 1994 sparked vast changes across the secretive communist country.

Markets are springing up in the shadows of abandoned factories, foreign influences are breaching the borders, inflation is soaring and corruption is rampant. A small nouveau riche class has emerged, even as a far larger group has been forced to trade away everything for food.

This is the picture of life in North Korea as painted by more than 30 people from Chongjin, the nation's third-largest city. Some are defectors living in South Korea. Others were interviewed in China, which they had entered illegally to work or beg. Accounts of aid workers and videos taken illegally in Chongjin by disgruntled residents were also used to prepare this report.

Although the North Korean regime has a reputation as the ultimate Big Brother, people from Chongjin say the public pays less and less heed to what the government says. There is little that might be called political dissent, but residents describe a pervasive sense of disillusionment that remains largely unspoken.

"People are not stupid. Everybody thinks our own government is to blame for our terrible situation," said a 39-year-old coal miner from Chongjin who was interviewed late last year during a visit to China. "We all know we think that, and we all know everybody else thinks that. We don't need to talk about it."

Kim Sun Bok, a 32-year-old former factory worker who came to South Korea last summer, said the country was "changing incredibly."

"It is not the same old North Korea anymore except in name."

Just a decade ago, when people in Chongjin needed new trousers, they had to go to government-owned stores that sold items mostly in drab browns or a dull shade of indigo. Food and other necessities

---

"People are not stupid. Everybody thinks our own government is to blame for our terrible situation."
—a North Korean coal miner from Chongjin

---

were rationed. Sometimes the government permitted the sale of home-grown vegetables, but even a hairbrush was supposed to be purchased from a state-run shop.

Today, people can shop at markets all over Chongjin, the result of a burst of entrepreneurship grudgingly allowed by the authorities. Almost anything can be purchased—ice cream bars from China, pirated DVDs, cars, Bibles, computers, real estate and sex—for those who can afford the high prices.

The retail mecca is Sunam market, a wood-frame structure with a corrugated tin roof that is squeezed between two derelict factories.

The aisles brim with fresh cucumbers, tomatoes, peaches, scallions, watermelons and cabbage, as shown by rare video footage taken last year by the Osaka, Japan-based human rights group Rescue the North Korean People. Everything else comes from China: belts, shoes, umbrellas, notebooks, plates, aluminum pots, knives, shovels, toy cars, detergents, shampoos, lotions, hand creams and makeup.

Each of Chongjin's seven administrative districts has a state-sanctioned market. Sunam, the city's largest, is expanding, and some say it has a wider variety of goods than the main market in Pyongyang. Many vendors wear their licenses pinned to their right breasts while the obligatory Kim Il Sung buttons remain over the heart.

Although markets have been expanding for more than a decade, it was only in 2002 and '03 that the government enacted economic reforms that lifted some of the prohibitions against them. Most of the vendors are older women such as Kim Hui Suk, a tiny 60-year-old with short, permed hair and immaculate clothing.

She was working in the day-care center of a textile factory in the early 1990s when production ground to a halt. Men were ordered to stay in their jobs, but Workers' Party cadres at the factory started whispering that the married women, or *ajumas*, ought to moonlight to provide for their families.

"It was clear that the *ajumas* had to go out and earn money or the family would starve," Kim said.

She first tried to raise pigs, locking them in a shed outside her downtown apartment building and feeding them slop left over from making tofu. But the electricity and water were too unreliable to keep the business going.

In 1995, Kim sold her apartment in the choice Shinam district and bought a cheaper one, hoping to use the proceeds to import rice from the countryside. But that too failed when she injured her back and couldn't work.

The family's situation became dire. Her husband's employer, a provincial radio station, stopped paying salaries, and food distribution ended. In 1996, her mother-in-law died of starvation, and her husband the following year.

"First he got really, really thin and then bloated. His last words to me were, 'Let's get a bottle of wine, go to a restaurant and enjoy ourselves,'" Kim recalled. "I felt bad that I couldn't fulfill his last wish."

In 1998, Kim's 26-year-old son, who had been a wrestler and gymnast, grew weak from hunger and contracted pneumonia. A shot of penicillin from the market would have cost 40 won, the same price as enough corn powder to feed herself and her three daughters for a week. She opted for the corn and watched her son succumb to the infection.

But Kim did not give up. She swapped apartments again and used the money to start another business, this time baking biscuits and *neungju*, a potent corn moonshine. If buyers didn't have cash, she would accept chile powder or anything else she could use.

"We made just enough to put food on the table," said Kim.

Much of Chongjin's commerce is still not officially sanctioned, so it has an impromptu quality. Money changes hands over wooden carts that can be rolled away in a hurry. Those who can't afford carts sell on tarpaulins laid out in the dirt.

Fashion boutiques are slapped together with poles and clotheslines, enlivening the monochromatic landscape with garish pinks and paisleys. Some clothes have the labels ripped out and vendors whisper that these items came from *araet dongne* or the "village below," a euphemism for South Korea, whose products are illegal in the North.

Shoppers can buy 88-pound sacks of rice emblazoned with U.S. flags, and biscuits and corn noodles produced by three factories in Chongjin run by the U.N. World Food Program—all intended to be humanitarian handouts.

Some people cut hair or repair bicycles, though furtively because these jobs are supposed to be controlled by the government's Convenience Bureau.

"They will bring a chair and mirror to the market to cut hair," Kim said. "The police can come at any moment, arrest them and confiscate their scissors."

Another new business is a computer salon. It looks like an Internet cafe, but because there's no access to the Web in North Korea, it is used mostly by teenagers to play video games.

More products are available, but inflation puts them out of reach for most people. The price of rice has increased nearly eightfold since the economic reforms of 2002 to 525 won per pound; an average worker earns 2,500 won a month—about $1 at the unofficial exchange rate.

World Food Program officials in North Korea say the vast majority of the population is less well off since the economic changes, especially factory workers, civil servants, retirees and anybody else on a fixed income. But there are those who have gotten rich. Poor Chongjin residents disparage them as *donbulrae*, or money insects.

"There are people who started trading early and figured out the ropes," said a 64-year-old retired math teacher who sells rabbits at the market. "But those of us who were loyal and believed in the state, we are the ones who are suffering."

If Chongjin's economic center is Sunam market, its political heart is Pohang Square, a vast plaza dominated by a 25-foot bronze statue of Kim Il Sung.

The grass here is neatly mowed, the shrubbery pruned and the pavement in good repair. Even when the rest of the city is without electricity, the statue is bathed in light. Across the street, a tidy pink building houses a permanent exhibit of the national flower, a hybrid begonia called *Kimjongilia*, named for current leader Kim Jong Il.

Since the practice of religion is barred, Pohang Square stands in as a spiritual center. Newlyweds in their best clothes pose for pictures, bowing to the statue so that their union is symbolically blessed.

When Kim Il Sung died on July 8, 1994, half a million people came to Pohang Square to pay their respects in the pouring rain and stifling heat. But among the adoring multitudes, there were malcontents.

One was Ok Hui, the eldest daughter of entrepreneur Kim Hui Suk. Though she dutifully took her place in the throng, any sadness she felt came from a foreboding that Kim Jong Il would be worse than his father.

"I went day and night along with everybody else. You had to. . . . But there were no tears coming from my eyes," recalled Ok Hui, now 39, who did not want her family name published.

Ok Hui worked for a construction company's propaganda unit, a job that entailed riding around in a truck with a megaphone, exhorting workers to do their best for the fatherland. But she didn't believe what she preached.

Her father had taught her to doubt the regime. As a reporter and member of the Workers' Party, he knew more about the outside world than many people and realized how far North Korea lagged behind South Korea and China.

"He and his friends would stay up at night when my mother was out, talking about what a thief Kim Jong Il was," Ok Hui said.

Her mother, though, remained a firm believer. "I lived only for the marshal. I never had a thought otherwise," said Kim Hui Suk. "Even when my husband and son died, I thought it was my fault."

Ok Hui and her mother frequently clashed. "Why did you give birth to me in this horrible country?" Ok Hui remembers taunting her mother.

"Shut up! You're a traitor to your country!" Kim retorted.

"Whom do you love more? Kim Jong Il or me?" her daughter shot back.

The regime was probably less beloved in Chongjin than elsewhere in North Korea. Food had run out in its province, North Hamgyong, earlier than in other areas, and starvation rates were among the highest in the nation.

Chongjin's people are reputed to be the most independent-minded in North Korea. One famous report of unrest centers on the city. In 1995, senior officers from the 6th army corps in Chongjin were executed for disloyalty and the entire unit, estimated at 40,000 men, was disbanded. It is still unclear whether the incident was an attempted uprising or a corruption case.

Chongjin is known for its vicious gang wars, and it was sometimes difficult to distinguish political unrest from ordinary crime. There were increasing incidents of theft and insubordination. At factories, desperate workers dismantled machinery or stripped away copper wiring to sell for food.

Public executions by firing squad were held outside Sunam market and on the lawn of the youth park, once a popular lover's lane.

In a village called Ihyon-ri on the outskirts of Chongjin, a gang suspected of anti-government activities killed a national security agent who had tried to infiltrate the group, former kindergarten teacher Seo Kyong Hui said.

"This guy was from my village. He had been sent to inform on a group that was engaged in suspicious activities," she said. "They caught him and stoned him to death."

Work crews went out early in the morning to wash away any anti-regime graffiti painted overnight, according to human rights groups, but most people were too scared to express their discontent. Badmouthing the leadership is still considered blasphemy.

To discourage anti-regime activity, North Korea punishes "political crimes" by banishing entire families to remote areas or labor camps.

"If you have one life to live, you would gladly give it to overthrow this government," said Seo, the teacher. "But you are not the only one getting punished. Your family will go through hell."

Even as Kim Jong Il's regime weakens, many of its stalwarts are growing richer. Many of Chongjin's well-to-do are members of the Workers' Party or are connected to the military or security services. In the new economy, they use their ties to power to trade with China, obtain market licenses, extract bribes and sell bureaucratic favors.

"Those who have power in North Korea always figure out ways to make money," said Joo Sung Ha, 31, who grew up in Chongjin and now works as a journalist in Seoul.

Joo was the pampered only son of a prominent official, and his family lived in Shinam, in the city's northern hills overlooking the ocean. By the standards of South Korea or China, the single-family homes with lines of fish and squid drying from the roofs are nothing special. But for North Koreans, these are mansions.

The Joo family had a 2,000-square-foot cement-block house and a walled garden about twice that large. The garden proved crucial in protecting the family against the famine, though they had to contend with hungry soldiers who would scale the walls and steal potatoes and cabbages.

North Korean families like to measure their status by the number of wardrobes they own, and Joo's family had five—plus a television, a refrigerator, a tape recorder, a sewing machine, an electric fan and a camera. They didn't have a phone or a car—at that time those were unthinkable even for a well-off family—but they did have a bicycle.

"The appliances were of no use after the electricity ran out," Joo said. "The bicycle was the most important thing, because the buses and trams stopped running."

Joo attended the best elementary school in Chongjin, the city's foreign language institute, and eventually the country's top school, Kim Il Sung University in Pyongyang. He never met a native English speaker in the North, or any foreigner for that matter, but he trained his ear with videotapes of the BBC and banned Hollywood films.

"I sometimes watched 'Gone With the Wind' twice a day. Anybody else would have been arrested for watching Hollywood movies," he recalled.

Joo's glimpses of Western culture eroded his loyalty to the system. "I saw myself 20 years down the road in the prime of my career and North Korea would be collapsing," he said.

While many of his classmates went to work for the regime's propaganda news service after graduating, Joo arranged to return to Chongjin, where he taught high school until he escaped in 2001.

"The people from our neighborhood couldn't understand," said Joo, who stays in contact with his family. "They thought I had everything."

Kim Hye Young, an actress, was also a child of privilege. Her father, Kim Du Seon, was an official of a trading company that sold mushrooms and fish in China. He learned how to navigate the bureaucracy, using his connections with the army and security services.

"If one of [the officials] had a wedding in the family, they would come to me for a couple of cases of wine," the older Kim said.

As trade with China became more important, the family prospered. They took drives in a company car and ate at Chongjin's nicest restaurant.

Growing up, Kim showed a flair for theater, and through her acting became a member of the elite in her own right. Her best-known role was in a play called "The Strong and the Righteous," in which she portrayed a spy who sacrifices her life for North Korea.

When the production won first place in a Pyongyang drama festival in 1996, she got to meet Kim Jong Il. Still breathless with the memory, she said the leader shook her hand and gave her a fountain pen.

"I knew that I, as an actress, had an important role to promote the ideology of my country," Kim said.

Kim and her sisters were largely oblivious to the famine, and their mother said she took pains to shelter them.

"My daughters don't know to this day how many children in our neighborhood starved to death," said her mother, Choe Geum Lan. She also didn't tell them that their father, as a result of his business trips to China, had become increasingly pessimistic about North Korea's future.

In 1998, when Kim was home from Pyongyang on vacation, her parents told her the family was going to visit an aunt in Musan, a city near the Chinese border. It was not until they had crossed to the other side that Kim and her teenage sisters, were told they had defected.

Kim, now 29 and advertising toothpaste on South Korean television, is one of the few defectors who says she didn't want to leave.

"I was content with my life," she said.

Today, North Korea's elites are even better off, buying telephones for their homes and even cars.

"For $4,000 or $5,000, anybody can buy a car now. It used to be that you weren't allowed to register your own car. We couldn't dream of it," said Kim Yong Il, a defector from Chongjin who lives in Seoul.

Recently, he arranged to have a computer smuggled from China to his relatives in Chongjin. North Korea's state-run companies don't have computers, so they're eager to hire people who do. "If you have a computer, you can get a job," he said.

Visitors have been shocked to glimpse the new conspicuous consumption in Chongjin.

Jeung Young Tai, a South Korean academic who was in Chongjin delivering South Korean government aid, noticed a paunchy man standing in front of the Chonmasan Hotel next to a new Lexus.

And at a hot spring in Kyongsong, on the city's outskirts, he saw a woman carrying a lap dog—a striking sight in a country where there is so little food that the only pets usually are goldfish.

"You get the sense that there is a tremendous gap between rich and poor and that the gap is growing," Jeung said.

> [The homeless are] called kotchebi, or swallows, because they wander the streets and sometimes between towns in search of food.

The flip side, of course, is that the poor are getting poorer.

In Chongjin, those at the very bottom of the heap can be found at the train station.

The cavernous building boasts a large portrait of Kim Il Sung above the entrance and a granite-faced clock that rarely tells the right time. In front is a vast plaza crammed with people waiting for trains—sometimes for days, because the trains have no fixed schedules—and people waiting for nothing at all.

These are the homeless, many of them children. They're called *kotchebi*, or swallows, because they wander the streets and sometimes between towns in search of food. Many gravitate to Chongjin station, because it is a major hub and the travelers have more to give.

A video shot last year by a military official and sold to Japan's NTV television captured barefoot children near the station in torn, filthy clothing fighting over a nearly empty jar of kimchi. One boy scooted along the pavement on his buttocks; the narrator said his toes had been eaten away by frostbite.

Kim Hyok knows how easy it is for a child to end up at the station; he spent the better part of two years living there.

"If you can't find somebody or they left their home, chances are you can find them at the station," said Kim, now 23 and resettled in South Korea.

Kim's mother died when he was a toddler, and he was raised by his father, a party member and an employee of a military unit that sold fish in China. During his early childhood, Kim, his father and elder brother lived in relative comfort in a high-rise apartment in the Sunam district.

> As people embarked on increasingly desperate hunts for food, families broke apart.

When the government stopped handing out rations in 1993, Kim's father used his connections to place his sons in an orphanage 60 miles away.

Kim, who was about 12 at the time, wasn't sorry to be sent away. It was considered a privilege because the orphanages had food.

In 1997, just before his 16th birthday, Kim "graduated" from the orphanage. He caught a train back to Chongjin, but when he got to his neighborhood, things looked unfamiliar. The electricity was off. Many apartment buildings had no glass in the windows and appeared vacant.

Climbing the eight flights in pitch dark to his family's unit, he heard a baby crying and wondered whose it might be. Confused and scared, he knocked on the door.

A young couple opened the door and told him his father had moved long ago but left a message: Look for him at the train station.

The phenomenon of vagrancy is testament to how much North Korea has changed. Before the famine, the government controlled people's movements so strictly that they could not dream of visiting a relative in a nearby town without a travel permit, let alone selling their homes. Not showing up for work could bring a visit from police.

But as people embarked on increasingly desperate hunts for food, families broke apart. With few telephones and a barely functional postal service, parents and children became separated.

"People just started wandering around because they were hungry," Kim said. "They would sell their apartments for a few bags of rice."

Kim never found his father. He also never found his brother, who had left the orphanage a year earlier.

With no place to go, Kim ended up at the train station. By night, he slept squeezed into a narrow space designed for a sliding iron gate. By day, he loitered near the food vendors on the plaza. He often worked with a gang of other kids—a few would topple a vendor's cart and the others would scoop up whatever spilled.

"If you're not fast, you can't eat," said Kim, who even today in South Korea bears the signs of chronic malnutrition, with a head that looks oversized on a shockingly short frame.

Kim began hopping the slow-moving trains that pass through Chongjin on their way to the Chinese border. Once on board, Kim would scramble up to the top of a car, flatten himself to avoid the electric lines above and, using his pack as a pillow, ride for hours.

At the border, he would wade across the river to hawk the items in his pack: household goods on consignment from Chongjin residents, who were selling off their possessions.

In 1998, Kim was arrested by Chinese authorities, who do not recognize North Koreans as refugees. He was sent back to North Korea and spent two years in a prison camp before escaping again in 2000 to China, where he was eventually taken in by missionaries and brought to South Korea.

For every homeless person who survived, many more likely died. Kim Hui Suk recalled a particularly ghoulish scene at the train station.

"Once I saw them loading three bodies into a cart," Kim said. "One guy, a man in his 40s, was still conscious. His eyes were sort of blinking, but they still were taking him away."

Although the ranks of the homeless have thinned since the height of the famine, North Korean residents say their numbers are still considerable.

"If somebody disappears, you don't know whether he dropped dead on the road or went to China," the coal miner said.

About 100,000 North Koreans have escaped to China in the last 10 years. Many have ended up returning to North Korea, either because they were deported or because they missed their families. They often back bring money, goods to trade and strange new ideas.

Smugglers carry chests that can hold up to 1,000 pirated DVDs. South Korean soap operas, movies about the Korean War and Hollywood action films are among the most popular. Even pornography is making its way in.

This is a radical change for a country so prudish that until recently women were not permitted to ride bicycles because it was thought too provocative. Seo Kyong Hui, the kindergarten teacher, said that when she left North Korea in 1998, "I was 26 years old, and I still didn't know how a baby was conceived."

Even today, women are prohibited from wearing short skirts or sleeveless shirts, and both sexes are forbidden to wear blue jeans. Infractions bring rebukes from the public standards police.

But it is a losing battle to maintain what used to be a hermetic seal around the country. Just a few years ago, ordinary North Koreans could make telephone calls only from post offices. Dialing abroad was virtually impossible. Now some people carry Chinese cellphones and pay for rides to the border to pick up a signal and call overseas.

Smugglers also bring in cheap Chinese radios. Unlike North Korean radios, which are preset to government channels, the Chinese models can be tuned to anything, even South Korean programs or the Korean-language broadcasts of Radio Free Asia.

In the past, being caught with such contraband would land a person in political prison. Nowadays, security personnel will more likely confiscate the illicit item for personal use.

When a policeman caught Ok Hui, the entrepreneur's daughter, with a Chinese radio in 2001, the first question he asked was, "So how do you work this thing?"

She wrote down the frequencies for South Korean radio stations.

"Don't you have earphones so you can listen without anybody hearing you?" the officer then demanded.

North Korea instructs its citizens that the country is a socialist paradise, but the government knows outside influences can puncture its carefully crafted illusions.

"Bourgeois anti-communist ideology is paralyzing the people's sound mind-set," warns a Workers' Party document dated April 2005. "If we allow ourselves to be affected by these novel ideas, our absolute idolization for the marshal [Kim Il Sung] will disappear."

Among those who make it to China, many describe a moment of epiphany when they find out just how bad off North Koreans are.

Kim Ji Eun, a doctor from Chongjin, remembers wading across the partially frozen Tumen River in March 1999, staggering to a Chinese farmhouse and seeing a dish of white rice and meat set out in a courtyard.

"I couldn't figure it out at first. I thought maybe it was for refrigeration," recalled Kim, who now lives in South Korea. "Then I realized that dogs in China live better than even party members in North Korea."

Many Chongjin residents who are caught trying to flee the country end up back in the city, behind the barbed wire of Nongpo Detention Center.

It sits near the railroad tracks in a swampy waterfront area. Prisoners are assigned back-breaking jobs in the nearby rice paddies or brick factory, where the workday begins at 5 a.m.

Ok Hui was one of those who served time in Nongpo. A rebel by nature, she had become fed up with North Korea and a difficult marriage.

In September 2001, during one of several failed attempts to escape, she was arrested in Musan and brought back to Chongjin by train. Guards tied the female prisoners to one another by tightly winding shoelaces around their thumbs.

In Nongpo, the inmates bunked in rows of 10, squeezed so tightly together that they had to sleep on their sides. Newcomers sometimes had to bed down in the corridor near overflowing toilets. Meals consisted of a thin, salty soup, sometimes supplemented by a few kernels of raw corn or a chunk of uncooked potato.

"The walls were very high and surrounded by wire," Ok Hui said. "One woman tried to climb the wall. They beat her almost to death. You can't imagine. They made us stand and watch."

One day, when she was assigned to work in the fields, she spotted an old woman. She took off her underwear and offered it to the woman in exchange for sending a message to her mother. Underwear is scarce in North Korea, so the woman accepted and agreed to send a telegram to Ok Hui's mother.

With her market earnings, Kim Hui Suk bought 10 packs of cigarettes for a security official to arrange her daughter's release.

Some days later, the prison administrator came to talk to Ok Hui and other female prisoners who were picking corn. They were all due to be freed shortly, and the administrator urged them to resist the temptations of capitalism and imperialism, and to devote themselves to North Korea.

Then, he asked for a show of hands: Who would promise not to run away again to China?

Not a single woman raised her arm.

"We were all just thinking that our whole lives we had been told lies," Ok Hui recalled. "Our whole lives, in fact, were lies. We just felt this immense rage toward the system."

The prison administrator looked at the women squatting sullenly in silence in the cornfield.

"Well," he said, "if you go again to China, next time don't get caught."

III. RELIEF EFFORTS: AID VERSUS DEVELOPMENT

Editor's Introduction

Many factors can contribute to food crises, but an actual lack of food in the world is not one of them. International agriculture produces enough to provide every person on Earth with at least 2,720 calories each day, far more than is needed to sustain life. People starve because they do not have access to food, not because adequate resources do not exist. This is where relief agencies come in, transferring some of the world's excess supply to locations where there are shortages. But while food aid may keep a family from starving, it alone cannot break the cycle that causes famine. Indeed, as the articles in this chapter, "Relief Efforts: Aid Versus Development," show, increased emphasis is being placed on the need for sustainable development practices in famine-prone countries.

The United States first officially established an international food aid program with the Agricultural Trade Development and Assistance Act of 1954. However, the country's history as an important worldwide donor nation began much earlier, in the aftermath of World War I. In "Fighting World Hunger: U.S. Food Aid Policy and the Food for Peace Program," the first article in this chapter, Ryan Swanson details the history of American food aid from World War I through the present.

The majority of other donor nations procure their aid locally in an attempt not only to feed the starving, but also to bolster the regional agricultural economy. However, the United States currently sends American crops overseas via American shipping companies. Frederic Mousseau and Anuradha Mittal examine this controversial policy in "Food Sovereignty: Ending World Hunger in Our Time," ultimately concluding that the American approach favors its own economy to the detriment of those whom it seeks to help. In the accompanying sidebar, "Localized Food Aid" by Alexandra Starr, Starr emphasizes the need to obtain food from local sources as a means of promoting long-term development, rather than using crops from abroad for temporary relief.

Publicity, relief agencies have learned, makes all the difference in generating money to deal with a food crisis. But the media does not typically cover a shortage until it has become a famine, and by then relief is considerably more costly. An author for the *Economist* explores this paradox, specifically as it relates to the media's impact on fundraising, in the fourth entry in this chapter, "Starving for the Cameras." In the following article, "Vast Lands, Epic Journeys, Terrible Sights," James R. Peipert reflects on his own experience as a reporter in Africa to explain why certain crises receive the media coverage they need to generate aid while others do not. Journalists, he writes, have limited resources to pursue stories, and much of famine-stricken Africa—lacking good infrastructure such as roads and airports, as well as reliable telecommunications for reporters to file stories—is not conducive to thorough news coverage. Nonetheless, when media outlets are willing to make the investment in a story, the benefits for that region are immense.

Finally, in "The Problem with Predicting Famine," Miren Gutierrez reports that anticipating famine is actually a relatively easy task, one that is ably performed by the Famine Early Warning Systems Network (FEWS NET) and the Global Information and Early Warning System (GIEWS). What is difficult is actually preventing an expected famine from taking place. The World Food Program, a UN agency, is primarily responsible for preventing food crises, but funding for the organization is in short supply and often materializes only once a formerly manageable shortage has reached crisis levels.

In the final pair of articles—"When Food Aid Doesn't Solve Africa's Problems" by Edgar R. Batte and the accompanying sidebar "Localized Food Aid" by Alexandra Starr—the authors emphasize the need to obtain food aid from local sources as a means of promoting long-term development, rather than using crops from abroad as a source of temporary relief.

Fighting World Hunger

U.S. Food Aid Policy and the Food for Peace Program

BY RYAN SWANSON
AGEXPORTER, OCTOBER 2004

The numbers are startling. More than 800 million people go to bed hungry each night, and nearly 50 million people currently face acute hunger as a result of war, civil strife or natural disaster. Additionally, the United Nations estimates that malnutrition is a significant factor in the deaths of 11,000 children each day.

Even in the 21st century, with its technological advances, the quest for food security remains a daunting challenge. There is some reason for optimism, however, as the United States and many other countries have put in place programs to fight hunger throughout the world and significant success has been achieved. But even with these victories, there is still much work yet to be done.

Although fertile soil and proficient farmers have consistently provided for the United States' domestic food needs, U.S. leaders have long recognized that the problem of food scarcity knows no national borders. On one hand, basic humanitarianism demands that hunger elsewhere cannot be simply ignored. But also, and perhaps more practically speaking, today's international economy determines that problems rarely stay confined to one particular country or region. The reverberations of food scarcity in one country make their impact felt in food markets around the world. The U.S. government designates millions of dollars and tons of food each year for food aid.

The United States has a long history of providing assistance to needy countries around the world. Following World War I, the American Relief Administration, led by entrepreneur and soon-to-be President Herbert Hoover, distributed more than 4 million tons of food and supplies to starving people in Europe, especially the Soviet Union. The Berlin Airlift of 1948 came in response to Joseph Stalin's closure of all roads and railroads into Berlin in June 1948. For nearly one year, British and American forces responded by delivering by plane all food and other necessary materials to sustain the isolated city. The delivery of over 500,000 tons of food eventually broke Stalin's blockade.

Although food aid programs currently enjoy widespread political support, it took a war to open the eyes of many politicians regarding their importance. World War II pushed the United States to

Article by Ryan Swanson from *AgExporter* October 2004. Article in public domain.

increase and formalize its food aid efforts. Throughout the years of fighting, Congress approved the donation of thousands of tons of food to European allies, especially the Soviet Union, to support both their armies and civilians. These food donations saved thousands of lives as famine spread throughout Europe. Following the war, U.S. involvement in food aid efforts continued to increase. The Marshall Plan, totaling nearly $13 billion, focused on feeding victims of the war and rebuilding the infrastructure and economy of Western Europe and Japan.

It was through this Plan, named for Secretary of State George C. Marshall, that U.S. government and military leaders first gained valuable experience in distributing food aid to destitute people. These leaders demonstrated to American politicians that a massive aid program could benefit both recipients and givers.

Chief among these rising leaders was a young army officer named Gwynn Garnett. Garnett served as the director of food and agriculture in the American zone of Germany and, on a daily basis, oversaw the procurement and distribution of extraordinary amounts of food to needy citizens. In this role, Garnett solidified an idea that changed U.S. food aid. Garnett proposed that the United States accept foreign currencies, many of which were virtually worthless outside their own borders after the war, in exchange for U.S. agricultural products. Although this approach seemed to suggest that the United States take a "loss" on its exports, Garnett focused on the larger ramifications.

The United States could use the local currency to rebuild the infrastructure and markets of war-ravaged areas that needed food. The United States could also fund the donation of food to the truly destitute. This investment would, in turn, facilitate the reopening of valuable markets for U.S. producers.

Leaders in both the Eisenhower Administration and Congress quickly embraced Garnett's plan when he presented it upon returning from Germany to serve as an American Farm Bureau official. The plan proved to be popular on two levels. It provided a structure by which the United States could meet the growing food needs of the world, and it helped put surplus U.S. agricultural production to good use.

The Foreign Agricultural Service and Food for Peace

The Agricultural Trade Development and Assistance Act of 1954 stamped Congress' approval on Garnett's plan. After the passage of P.L. (Public Law) 480 in July 1954, USDA received its marching orders. The law provided the means to offer needy countries low-interest, long-term credit to purchase U.S. agricultural goods. The President delegated the concessional credit authority under that Act to the Secretary of Agriculture, who redelegated that authority to FAS.

P.L. 480, which has six program titles, continues 50 years after its origin to be the backbone of the United States' diverse food aid effort. Administered by FAS, Title I makes available long-term, low-interest credit to needy countries so that they may purchase U.S. agricultural commodities. Title I allows the long-term debt acquired under P.L. 480 to be repaid in the currency of the borrowing country; however, since the early 1970s, P.L. 480 debt has been repaid in U.S. dollars.

For countries where even the most generous credit terms are too heavy an economic burden, U.S. efforts take a different approach. Title II of P.L. 480, administered by USAID (the U.S. Agency for International Development), allows for the outright donation of U.S. agricultural commodities to meet humanitarian needs around the world. Donations can be distributed through government agencies, private charities or international organizations such as the WFP (World Food Program).

Commodities are currently obtained by purchase from private producers or from stocks held by USDA's CCC (Commodity Credit Corporation). In addition, the Title II program pays the transport, storage and distribution costs associated with the donations.

Title III of P.L. 480, the Food for Development program, is currently inactive. Also administered by USAID, it provides government-to-government assistance grants to least-developed countries to support development.

> U.S. food aid policy evolved continuously as new needs arose, new challenges cropped up, and different presidential administrations placed their stamp on aid efforts.

Drawing on a Heritage of Aiding the Needy

P.L. 480 built upon the Agricultural Act of 1949, which allowed excess commodities held by the CCC to be distributed outside the United States when the need arose. In 1951 alone, Congress acted to help Yugoslavia and India through times of famine. The Yugoslav Emergency Relief Assistance Act in 1951 had particular significance because it sent an important message of support to Yugoslavia as it broke ties with the Soviet Union.

As is the case with most legislation, the true impact of P.L. 480 became evident as details became codified and action commenced. Initially, politicians argued over how exactly the program would function. Senator Hubert Humphrey, in particular, championed the idea that P.L. 480 must emphasize the donation of food to needy countries, and that such efforts must not exist only as a side-note to surplus commodity disposal. In his 1958 Congressional report entitled "Food and Fiber as a Force for Freedom," Humphrey took issue with farmers who he felt were interested only in surplus reallocation for the benefit of American agriculturalists.

Eventually, President Dwight D. Eisenhower pursued a middle road that took into consideration both the plight of American farmers and the vast potential of food diplomacy. The President supported Humphrey's call for P.L. 480 to be known as the "Food for Peace program," and in 1960 established both the position of Food for Peace Coordinator and the Office of Food for Peace.

U.S. food aid policy evolved continuously as new needs arose, new challenges cropped up, and different presidential administrations placed their stamp on aid efforts. In 1961, President John F. Kennedy established USAID. The new Agency partnered with FAS in the disbursal of food aid throughout the world, and it continues to administer Title II distributions. In 1962, in response to appeals that had been made by both Eisenhower and Kennedy, the United Nations established its WFP. At the suggestion of Senator George McGovern, who was then the White House Director of the U.S. Food for Peace program, the WFP began initially on a three-year trial basis before rapidly assuming a permanent, leading role in the fight to reduce hunger.

The Food Aid Convention of 1967 brought the question of how to confront world hunger to the forefront of international relations. For the first time, the United States and 11 other developed countries

---

Food aid policy must be carefully constructed in order to preserve the normal flow of trade and to limit any price impact on agricultural commodities.

---

gathered to discuss their mutual commitments to food aid. The participating government leaders reached a formal agreement that set minimum levels of food support for needy countries each year, regardless of surpluses or commodity prices that might be in effect. The United States assumed by far the largest responsibility, originally providing over 75 percent of the commodities donated, but a precedent of international cooperation was established.

Ever-Increasing Challenges

As support for food aid policies has expanded, logistical challenges have increased as well. Early FAS and USAID administrators faced the challenge of deciding which countries should be served; how excess commodities should be obtained; and which commodities were most suitable nutritionally. Other questions, such as how the cost of transport should be met and how aid should be distributed without altering the world trade balance, also presented significant challenges.

Food aid policy must be carefully constructed in order to preserve the normal flow of trade and to limit any price impact on agricultural commodities. FAS officials closely observe usual marketing requirements, mandating that countries receiving aid continue to trade even as they receive outside assistance. FAS prohibits the resale of P.L. 480 Title I commodities to third countries. P.L. 480 Title I requires that all purchases go through a rigorous bidding system. The recipient governments make the purchases. FSA (the Farm Service Agency) of USDA purchases commodities for Title II using an open competitive process. Additionally, P.L. 480 protects the ability of small businesses to participate by disallowing minimum order levels under Title II. These rules exist to create competition and integrity on the supply side in order that food aid needs can be met as efficiently and prudently as possible.

New challenges arise each year. Recently, U.S. efforts to assist countries in need of food have been plagued by controversy over the use of biotechnology. FAS and USAID officials have taken on the role of educator as they explain why and how this technology is used. Adding to the changes, the scope of food aid has continued to evolve. The new goal of food security encompasses more than just donations in times of crisis. Rather, "food security" focuses on the access by all people at all times to sufficient food for active, healthy lives.

Adaptation and Flexibility—the Keys to Continued Success

Because of the constantly changing landscape of food needs around the world, U.S. food aid policy has come to be characterized by continual evolution of many different programs. While P.L. 480 still functions quite effectively, the U.S. government has added new programs to address previously unforeseen situations. In the 1980s, food aid officials recognized that in order for the United States to have the freedom to address pressing international needs as they arise, an adequate reserve was needed. A commodity reserve, originally authorized by the Agricultural Trade Act of 1980 and now known as the Bill Emerson Humanitarian Trust, serves that purpose by allowing the United States to store up to 4 million metric tons of wheat, corn, sorghum and rice, to be used in case of a food emergency or to otherwise meet P.L. 480 program needs in a tight supply situation. The Secretary of Agriculture has authority to release up to 500,000 tons of grain each year for emergency assistance.

Numerous times throughout the 1980s and 1990s, presidents have released grain from the Trust in response to difficult circumstances. In 1984, President Ronald Reagan authorized the release of 300,000 tons of grain to help fight widespread famine in Africa. Presidents George H. W. Bush and Bill Clinton designated the release of grain to aid the Middle East and the Caucasus regions. In 2002, officials released 275,000 tons of grain to again aid starving people in Southern Africa. The drought in that region created a situation of unexpected severity, the type of unpredictable calamity that the Emerson Trust was intended to hedge against. The fund currently has a balance of over 2 million tons.

In the 1980s, another significant new food aid program emerged, this one with a more concerted diplomatic focus. The Food for Progress initiative, first authorized in 1985, made very explicit the connection between the donation of food and the recipient country's philosophy of government. Commodities came from CCC stocks or purchases from the market and may be furnished in the form of either financing or donations.

But most significantly, Food for Progress did just what its title suggested—it linked food and progress. Only countries that were emerging democracies or that made a significant commitment to free enterprise in their agricultural economies could receive aid under this provision.

Food for Progress donations have been made to countries all over the world. In 1999, for example, after Hurricane Mitch nearly crippled Honduras and Nicaragua, FAS, through the Food for Progress program, made direct food donations valued in excess of $13.5 million. The donations eased the hunger caused by the hurricane and helped with the rebuilding of the agricultural infrastructure in those countries.

Like the Food for Progress initiative, the most recent addition to the United States' array of food aid programs seeks to improve the societal conditions of the receiving country. In July 2000, President Bill Clinton committed the United States to providing resources worth $300 million to help establish school nutrition programs in needy countries. Strongly backing this move were two long-time proponents of food aid and increased school nutrition programs, Senators George McGovern and Robert Dole. In 2001, the pilot Global Food for Education Initiative began distributing commodities via the WFP as well as through many private voluntary organizations.

In the course of a two-year trial, the program provided nutritional meals for nearly 7 million children in 38 countries. The goal was not only to abate hunger, but also to increase the number of children who attend school. It is estimated that 120 million school-age children currently do not attend school because of lack of food and proper nutrition. Many are forced to work in the fields to maintain even a subsistence lifestyle.

This new initiative gained permanent status under the 2002 Farm Security and Rural Investment Act. As a result of the legislation, the McGovern-Dole International Food for Education and Child Nutrition Program was launched in 2003 to provide school meals, teacher training and technological support to foreign countries. The program will take different forms in different countries. In Eritrea, for example, plans call for a joint program to be conducted through Africare and Mercy Corps International to provide 65,000 students with high-protein biscuits and milk throughout the school year. In Guatemala, Catholic Relief Services and World Share will take profits made from selling U.S. goods and use them to purchase locally grown food in order to supplement students' diets. In addition to the program flexibility that allows different organizations to distribute aid, the McGovern-Dole program also pays transport and shipping costs.

Undoubtedly, new challenges will arise in the coming years. Changes in technology, the environment and the economy will cause food aid policy-makers to seek new ways to help feed the hungry around the world. But the legacy of U.S. efforts such as Food for Peace and Food for Progress will provide a strong foundation to continue to work toward food security for the world's most vulnerable citizens.

Food Sovereignty

Ending World Hunger in Our Time

BY FREDERIC MOUSSEAU AND ANURADHA MITTAL
THE HUMANIST, MARCH/APRIL 2006

This past Thanksgiving, while millions of Americans sat at a table overflowing with food, more than thirty children died each minute around the world due to hunger related causes.

Certainly hunger isn't a result of food scarcity. In fact, *abundance* best describes the world's food supply. World agriculture produces 17 percent more calories per person today than it did thirty years ago, despite a 70 percent population increase. This is enough food to provide every person worldwide with at least 2,720 kilocalories a day.

International food aid, the most publicized instrument in the campaign against hunger, was initiated in 1954, and yet hunger is a bigger crisis now than ever before. Chronic hunger affects over 852 million people across the globe, and its victims include 6.5 million children who die from hunger related causes each year—one every five seconds. While millions of tons of food are shipped as food aid to the global south, apart from some specific disaster and war situations, this doesn't serve the hungry and malnourished whose numbers increase by 4.5 million each year.

So who then benefits the most from food aid? Specific crop lobbies, U.S. shipping companies, and NGO and relief organizations are some of the top winners. For example, Horizon Milling, a joint venture of Cargill Inc. and CHS Inc., has since 1995 sold to the U.S. government $1.09 billion of grain for food aid operations. The second player, the shipping industry, is supported by the 1985 Farm Bill, which requires that at least 75 percent of U.S. food aid be shipped by U.S. vessels. And the main U.S.–based relief and development organizations rely highly on in-kind U.S. food aid for either direct food interventions or for funding of other activities. On average the main U.S.–based relief groups rely on the sale of food aid in developing countries for 30 percent of their resources.

This preferential treatment to food produced in the United States and for U.S. shipping companies makes U.S. food aid the most expensive in the world. The premiums paid to suppliers and shippers raise the cost of food aid by over 100 percent compared to local

"Food Aid or Food Sovereignty? Ending World Hunger in Our Time," The Oakland Institute, 2005. *www.oaklandinstitute.org*.

purchases. As reported in the *New York Times*, food delivered by NGOs and the World Food Program (WFP) in 2004 cost only 40 percent of the U.S. food aid budget. The rest was pocketed by suppliers.

In addition, this requirement delays delivery of emergency food aid by an average of nearly five months. In fact, most times, aid is too little and too late. It was appalling to see images of victims of starvation in Niger hit the Western media in July 2005, when the food shortage had been announced nearly a year before without triggering a response that could have prevented or ameliorated a famine. The severity of the situation was known in October 2004 when Niger's government and the WFP appealed for international support. Four months after its first appeal WFP had received only 10 percent of the required funding. According to Jan England, humanitarian coordinator for the United Nations, in October 2004 $1.00 per day could save a child's life whereas $80.00 dollars per day was required in July 2005.

Recognizing this, the European Union procures a majority of its food aid—90 percent in 2004—from developing countries. Canada

---

Food aid needs drastic changes if we really want to diminish world hunger.

---

increased local and regional purchases from 10 percent to 50 percent in September 2005. The United States is the only donor nation that has avoided local and regional purchases.

The White House and USAID have proposed to spend in 2006 one quarter of its food aid budget to buy food grown by local or regional producers. However, both House and Senate leaders have rejected this recommendation. Virginia Republican Bob Goodlatte, chair of the House Agriculture Committee, has gone on to warn that buying food aid overseas would erode congressional support for famine-fighting programs: "It must come from American farmers so it will circulate through the American economy." Instead of prioritizing feeding starving stomachs, Congress' focus remains fixed on fattening pockets of agribusiness and shipping companies.

A joint poll conducted by the *Washington Post*, Harvard University, and the Kaiser Family Foundation asked Americans which area of federal expenditure they thought was the largest. Sixty-four percent of the respondents said it was foreign aid, which in fact constitutes less than one half of one percent of the federal budget. Their response isn't surprising, though, given the number of people who are generously contributing to relief efforts from New Orleans to Niger. But Americans could do even more by challenging the lawmakers who have been blinded by corporate America's interests.

Food aid needs drastic changes if we really want to diminish world hunger. If kept separate from trade and other political interests and supported by a consistent aid budget, the replacement of in-kind food aid with local and triangular purchases would double the amount of food available. The current U.S. food aid budgets could be cut in half without a decrease in the overall volume delivered if the food were procured locally.

More importantly, a study on food aid—*Food Aid or Food Sovereignty? Ending World Hunger in Our Time*—conducted recently by the Oakland Institute, shows that while the European and Canadian shift to local purchases is good it doesn't necessarily promote food security in developing countries. The study recommends that, first, local procurement of food aid must prioritize small-scale farmers, given the dumping of subsidized food as aid adversely affects local agricultural capacity and erodes farmers' livelihoods.

Since most low-income, food-deficit countries (LDCs) specialize in non-food exportable commodities like coffee, cocoa, tea, and tobacco, the top ten list of WFP suppliers include, instead of LDCs, a number of "more advanced" developing countries, such as Brazil and South Africa, which specialize in industrial production of exportable food commodities. For example, in 2005 South Africa will be the origin of most WFP purchases for interventions in Southern Africa, and triangular purchases will consist of cereals produced by large-scale commercial farmers and agribusinesses. Small-scale farmers in Mozambique will also produce a surplus in 2005, yet they are unlikely to supply food to the WFP because of higher marketing costs due to the country's poor road and storage infrastructure.

Another factor that requires emphasis be put on purchases from small farmers locally is the fact that large companies dominate export trade in developing countries. Two corporations—Cargill, the United States' largest privately owned corporation and Archer Daniels Midland (ADM)—control 75 percent of the global grain trade. These corporations dominate the agricultural sector of many developing countries. For instance, Nestlé controls 80 percent of milk production in Peru. Cargill Paraguay sells more than 30 percent of the total production of soy, wheat, and corn of the country.

In the aftermath of the devastating tsunami that struck Indonesia in 2004, local farmers groups organized a farmer's network to supply fresh food to the affected populations of Banda Aceh, demonstrating the feasibility of addressing acute emergency needs with food produced locally by small producers. In the West Bank, WFP buys olive oil from destitute farmers who have been cut off from their markets by the separation wall. This type of local purchase requires flexible and decentralized procurement systems and eventually benefits local agriculture and reduces the need for food aid in the long run.

Second, donors must not only review their procurement system and dissociate food aid from their national interests but also increase the amount of resources for agriculture and rural development which have been cut by half from $5.14 billion to $2.22 billion in the past two decades. Examples from situations of extreme hunger around the world have proven that, in the long run, policies that emphasize helping affected countries develop their own agricultural sectors actually help feed more people and decrease developing countries' dependence on aid programs.

Third, it is essential that strategies are put in place to reduce food aid needs over the long term. This requires support for national policies that are built on the foundation of food sovereignty and support small farmers through land redistribution, extension services, and support for the production of staple food rather than cash crops. In addition, the protection of prices and markets and the management of national food stocks will be essential to mitigate the effects of the fluctuations of national food production on producers and consumers, thereby reducing the need for food aid.

Under the dictates of the international financial institutions, marketing boards, which stabilized prices and managed national food stocks, have been systematically dismantled in many developing countries. These state-run institutions emphasized self-sufficiency, thereby reducing the need for food imports. This allowed governments to buy agricultural commodities from farmers, keep them in a rolling stock, and release them into the market in the event of a bad harvest in the following years. Marketing boards also organized the redistribution of food from surplus to deficit areas of the country. Preventing price volatility, they protected both producers and consumers against sharp rises or drops in prices. Today in Niger or in Malawi, as pointed out by the humanitarian relief organization Doctors Without Borders, the root cause of hunger is poverty, and the group is distributing food to those who are too poor to buy food. In the absence of price controls, the poor have seen price increases of 100 to 200 percent during the lean periods.

During the 1990s Indonesia signed the General Agreement on Tariffs and Trade (GATT) which reduced state intervention in food production and opened up domestic markets to foreign imports. By the end of the 1990s Indonesia became a large importer of rice and one of the largest recipients of food aid. In 2002 the government reintroduced tariffs and imposed tighter control on rice imports. Bulog, the state agency whose role had shrunk in the 1990s, was again put in charge of stabilizing the market and acting as a safety net. Decentralized and operating countrywide, the agency not only supplied the market with rice during lean seasons and periods of high prices but also redistributed surpluses to regions that encountered staple food deficits. In 2004 the country became self-sufficient in the production of rice for the first time in twenty years and had to ban imports to protect its market and producers.

Zimbabwe underwent a similar experience in the 1990s. Under structural adjustment, extreme poverty increased by 50 percent between 1990 and 1995. Recognizing that agricultural growth did not benefit the poor, but rather large-scale farmers and agribusinesses, the government decided to return its market and safety net function to its Grain Marketing Board, which had almost been eliminated following the recommendations of the International Monetary Fund and the World Bank. Affected by severe food shortages over the past three years, Zimbabwe has been able to import and distribute over one million tons of food through its board.

Some would say that this is an idealistic vision. But the world is desperate for answers. The worst is happening right now from Niger to Malawi. So the next time we sit down to an overflowing banquet we must face some simple questions: do we want freedom from hunger or freedom to trade? Do we want a corporate-profit steered world as that envisioned by Cargill and Continental or do we want strong native cultures proud of their ability to feed their people?

LOCALIZED FOOD AID

BY ALEXANDRA STARR
THE NEW YORK TIMES MAGAZINE, DECEMBER 11, 2005

In emergency medicine, doctors often refer to the "golden hour," or the 60-minute window after a medical calamity when treatment is most likely to save the patient. Famine emergencies have a similar dynamic: if food arrives at the earliest signs of a shortage, more lives will be saved. Buying food locally often provides the greatest chance to prevent starvation. That's partly because of the geography of famine relief. About two-thirds of countries in need are in Africa, while many of the donor countries are congregated in North America and Western Europe. Shipping emergency food aid from the U.S. often takes five months or longer.

Every country that contributes regularly to famine relief has the flexibility to buy locally, with the exception of the biggest donor: the United States. Federal laws more than half a century old dictate that all food aid has to be purchased in and shipped from U.S. soil. Earlier this year, the Bush administration tried to relax the rules and allow up to one-fourth of the food-aid budget to be used to buy commodities from in or around the famine-afflicted country. The proposal, however, was voted down in Congress.

The defeat could be chalked up to the fact that it ran afoul of a fundamental tenet of U.S. food aid: help the needy but also make sure you boost the bottom line of agribusiness and shipping companies. While it's understandable that corporations are loath to forfeit government money, they have a somewhat surprising ally in maintaining the status quo: nongovernmental organizations. These groups, which distribute food in poor countries, have their own financial stake in fighting local buying. That's because only a fraction of the food donated by U.S. farmers is used in famine emergencies. Development and relief groups sell the surplus and earmark the proceeds for anti-hunger and poverty programs. They fear that ending the current practice of shipping from the U.S. will curtail big-business support for food aid, leading to smaller budgets. Those, in turn, could jeopardize their anti-hunger programs.

Despite the poor reception that the Bush proposal received, there are signs that the U.S. will ultimately loosen its "buy American" policy. Some NGO's like CARE and Oxfam have come out in support of local buying. And European countries are leaning on the U.S. to change the current system, claiming it's a de facto agriculture export subsidy. For now, however, the golden hour in famine relief is likely to slip away before U.S. ships laden with food arrive on the scene.

Starving for the Cameras

Economist, August 18, 2005

The Famine Early Warning Systems Network, known as FEWS Net, monitors the threat of mass hunger in some of the poorest parts of the world. It is hardly surprising, then, that FEWS Net has published an inquiry into the world's failure to respond to food shortages in Niger and the rest of the Sahel. The report is subtitled simply: "What went wrong?" That is the right question to ask. But what is surprising, and disconcerting, is that the report was written in 1997, not 2005.

This illustrates two things: Niger's present nightmare is a recurring one; and whatever went wrong in 1997 was not put right by 2005. In both cases, signs of distress were recognised early, but the response was dilatory. In both cases, relief agencies and donors failed to settle on an assessment of need. The decisive difference is that, in 1997, the international media were largely absent. In 2005, by contrast, the drought of attention eventually turned into a deluge. The Niger appeal received more money in the ten days after the media arrived on the scene than it had in the previous ten months. As a result, the worst may now be over there.

Unfortunately, the media will always arrive late, if at all. Famine is a complex process, not a single, abrupt event. Food prices rise, families sell their assets, some migrate in search of work or wild foods. As hunger sets in, the body's own assets decline. It is only after stomach muscles have wasted that the distended bellies so sadly familiar from television pictures appear. These images have become necessary to the genre. The falling livestock prices that long preceded them are not as telegenic.

Hunger also prevails far beyond the media spotlight. According to FEWS Net, many more people are affected by continuing food crises in Ethiopia, Somalia, Zimbabwe and Sudan. In each of those countries, there are also many hungry and dying babies. But the bright light the media sheds on its chosen subject throws everything else into shadow.

The Bandwagon Dilemma

The media attention now devoted to Niger and the political weight it carries pose a tactical dilemma for the aid agencies. Do they slow the bandwagon down to try to redirect it to other destinations it might otherwise bypass? Or do they take advantage of the media spotlight to wring as much money out of donor governments as they can?

To downplay the crisis carries a big risk: there is a high political price to pay if one is seen as not doing enough in the face of such hardship. But

> Famine is preventable
> because it is predictable.

there are equal and opposite dangers. Inevitably, the media sometimes overstate things. Loose talk of famine and millions of starvation deaths can do more harm than good. Such talk can tempt private traders to hoard grain, either out of fear that they, too, will succumb to famine or out of greed, anticipating the higher prices an international relief effort will pay. Media reports may also have prompted Niger's neighbours, from which it normally buys food, to restrict exports of grain to the country.

Famine is preventable because it is predictable. The job of foreseeing it falls to the early warning systems, such as FEWS Net, which is funded by the American government, and its UN counterpart. The job of preventing it falls first and foremost to the World Food Programme, another UN agency, plus a long train of private agencies. The job of funding their efforts falls to no one in particular. But then, when the cameras arrive, it falls to everyone at once.

Last year, Hilary Benn, Britain's minister for international development, made two proposals that now look more timely than ever. The most obvious one is to establish a standing fund on which relief agencies can draw. Such a fund should not free these agencies from accountability to their donors. But it should spare them from the need to court their paymasters in a panicked response to every emergency.

Early interventions are not only cheaper than belated ones. They can also avoid some of the dangers of food aid. Cheap food dumped on local markets for long periods might save some from starvation, but it can also hurt farmers, perversely eroding a country's agricultural capacity in the name of food security. In Ethiopia, which in 2003 received food aid equivalent to 15% of its annual cereal production, agricultural yields have stagnated. An early intervention that arrives before people's livelihoods are destroyed and before they are too weak to work can offer cash or vouchers with which to buy food on the market, rather than emergency rations to keep them alive.

Mr. Benn's second proposal is that one agency, such as the European Commission's humanitarian agency ECHO, be designated a "financier of last resort," a kind of swing provider of aid, whose job is to cater to the crises every other donor neglects. Both proposals have merit. The world's system for fighting the direst cases of mass hunger should not rest on a global sympathy contest umpired by television cameras.

Vast Lands, Epic Journeys, Terrible Sights

BY JAMES R. PEIPERT
FORT WORTH STAR-TELEGRAM, AUGUST 28, 2005

Every few years, we in the comfortable, self-absorbed West sud-denly become aware of a famine or some other catastrophe afflicting a remote corner of Africa.

Almost overnight, it seems, newspapers, magazines and TV news-casts are replete with compelling images: skeletal children with distended abdomens, anguished parents, ramshackle refugee camps on barren plains.

The latest focus of Western interest is Niger, a West African country of meager resources that's relentlessly being swallowed by the Sahara Desert. During the past year, Niger has suffered a severe drought and a plague of locusts. Most of the country's subsis-tence crops were destroyed, and an estimated 3 million of Niger's 11.6 million people face starvation.

How can we help? Why didn't we know about this sooner? Why didn't you journalists write about this earlier?

These questions are inevitably asked as people in the developed world respond to a human impulse to share some of their bounty with those less fortunate. But the fact is that the world has no shortage of places in dire need. International aid agencies, some with workers on the ground, monitor such situations and issue peri-odic reports and pleas for help. But they get scant attention until a reporter shows up with a camera—preferably a TV camera.

Unfortunately, only a few of those places have the good luck to be visited by camera-toting reporters whose images might capture the fleeting attention of the West and perhaps trigger an outpouring of aid.

The Role of Serendipity

Getting to those needy places and getting word out to the world is often a serendipitous process. Reporters will ask such questions as: Where can we get to quickest? Can we get our film out? Will the gov-ernment try to stop us from covering the story? (In Niger, for exam-ple, President Mamadou Tandja has denied that his country is experiencing a famine and said that his people are well-fed.)

Even in an age of instant communications, vast reaches of the globe are far from the easy reach of reporters. Africa, for example, comprises 22 percent of the world's land area and stretches about 5,000 miles from Cairo to Cape Town. It could accommodate the United States, Europe, India and Japan and still have about 2 million square miles left over.

Niger, mostly desert plains and sand dunes with only about 500 miles of paved roads, is slightly less than twice the size of Texas. Sudan, Africa's biggest country, is about the size of the United States east of the Mississippi River.

With news resources concentrated on such major foreign stories as the Iraq war, the Israeli-Palestinian conflict and some of lesser world impact—such as the search for an Alabama teenager missing in Aruba—that immense African land mass gets short shrift.

Those foreign correspondents who actually live in Africa tend to be based in capitals where things work— at least most of the time. They need decent airline connections to allow quick access to breaking stories in coverage areas encompassing thousands of square miles. They also require reliable telecommunications to file the stories and sound banking systems to transfer funds from their home offices to run the news operations.

> Even in an age of instant communications, vast reaches of the globe are far from the easy reach of reporters.

Correspondents congregate in such places as Nairobi, Kenya, in East Africa; Johannesburg, South Africa; Cairo, Egypt, in the north; and perhaps Abidjan, Ivory Coast; or Lagos, Nigeria, in the west.

This time, the plight of a remote African nation was brought to Western consciousness by Hilary Andersson, a reporter for the British Broadcasting Corp. based in Johannesburg.

Kevin Bakhurst, editor of the BBC's flagship domestic news program, Ten O'Clock News, had asked Andersson to investigate reports from international aid agencies that a crisis was looming in Niger and other countries in sub-Saharan West Africa—Mali, Burkina Faso and Mauritania.

"When Hilary and the team got there, we were all shocked by what they found," Bakhurst was quoted as saying on the BBC Web site NewsWatch.

Andersson's first reports, including gripping film footage from Niger, were aired on the Ten O'Clock News during the week of July 17 and was picked up quickly by media outlets around the world.

Suddenly, as in the past, the world was aware of a crisis in Africa.

But just getting from South Africa to Niger's famine-devastated Maradi province, Andersson wrote, was an "epic journey."

"Our team left Johannesburg on a Tuesday, and arrived there in the evening three days later after flights all over Africa and a nine-hour drive through scorching desert," she wrote in an Aug. 2 report on the NewsWatch Web site.

"Our hotel in Maradi was virtually empty, we were the only foreign journalists there. In the world's eyes, Niger was just having another hard year."

But within a few days of the BBC reports, Andersson wrote, "Britain had doubled aid to Niger, aid began flowing in, the U.N. talked about how the power of television had woken up the world to Niger's crisis."

When Andersson's team left Maradi, to be relieved by a fresh BBC crew, "our hotel was so full of journalists and aid workers that there were no rooms left in the inn."

Echoes of the Past

Andersson's account recalled another famine, in another African country, in another time: Ethiopia in 1984–85. That famine killed an estimated 1 million people; the BCC described it in a 20th-anniversary perspective piece in 2004 as "the greatest natural disaster of the twentieth century."

I remember that one vividly.

At the time, I worked for The Associated Press as East Africa bureau chief, based in Nairobi. Our coverage area, a huge and diverse chunk of the continent, stretched from Ethiopia in the north to Zimbabwe in the south—almost as far from one end to the other as New York is from Los Angeles.

To us and other reporters in the region, the famine didn't come as a surprise. In the AP bureau, we had been writing about drought and famine in Ethiopia—and more than 20 other African countries—for well over two years.

Barry Shlachter, who then worked in the bureau and now is a business news reporter for the Star-Telegram, made two trips to Addis Ababa, the Ethiopian capital, early in 1984—once to report on an international conference of meteorologists who tried to gauge the impact of the drought.

But Shlachter was denied permission to leave the city to see first-hand the drought-afflicted regions in the north—not even for stories suggested by the government's own relief agency.

The Marxist regime of Col. Mengistu Haile Mariam was planning a gala celebration in September to mark the 10th anniversary of the overthrow of Emperor Haile Selassie on Sept. 12, 1974. Photographs of starving children in the world's media would hardly be a fitting testimonial to a decade of socialism under Mengistu's military junta.

Not until after the self-congratulatory glad-handing was over did the government allow foreign correspondents to travel to the north.

The BBC was the first in—thanks to the efforts of Mohamed Amin, a Nairobi-based cameraman who did TV work for the BBC and other TV news organizations, as well as shooting still pictures for the AP.

Amin, who had chronicled Africa for decades, used his contacts in Addis Ababa to arrange for the visit of the four-member BBC crew: Amin himself, Africa-based British correspondents Michael Buerk and Mike Wooldridge, and soundman Zack Njuguna.

After arrival in Addis Ababa, the four hitched a ride to the north aboard a Twin Otter aircraft operated by World Vision International, a Christian relief organization. They landed in Mekele, in the province of Tigre, on Oct. 19 and during the next few days traveled also to Alamata and Korem.

They were astounded by what they found.

"Dawn—and as the sun breaks through the piercing chill of night on a plain outside Korem, it lights up a biblical famine, now, in the twentieth century."

Those words opened Buerk's first report on the Ethiopian famine for BBC's Six O'Clock News on Oct. 23. Amin's footage was picked

---

The worldwide publicity generated by the famine brought on what became known locally as a "celebrity glut."

---

up by NBC later that day and shown in the United States at the end of the network's Nightly News.

On the morning of Oct. 23, just after Amin's return from Ethiopia, he and I spread out a selection of his best still photographs on a desk in AP's Nairobi bureau and selected five for transmission on the AP network. The pictures, showing shrouded bodies awaiting burial and hundreds of thousands waiting for food at relief centers, were used in AP member newspapers worldwide.

Within 36 hours of the initial reports, the relief organization Save the Children reported receiving more than 10,000 phone calls.

On Oct. 30, I flew from Nairobi to Addis Ababa without a visa or even a change of clothes, hitching a ride with Amin on a Lear jet chartered by a TV crew. With Amin pulling the right strings in Ethiopia's sometimes impenetrable bureaucracy, I managed to get a visa for a month. Shlachter relieved me at the end of November—to be followed by other AP reporters during the next six months.

Suddenly, the aid started to flow.

President Reagan authorized $45 million in U.S. emergency funding, saying he couldn't get Amin's images out of his head. Two Live Aid concerts—in London and Philadelphia—in the summer of 1985 were seen by an estimated billion people around the globe and raised tens of millions of dollars. Despite the animosities of the Cold War, U.S. and Soviet transport planes jockeyed for space on the gravel airstrip at Mekele and other feeding stations around Ethiopia.

"Celebrity Glut"

The worldwide publicity generated by the famine brought on what became known locally as a "celebrity glut"—politicians, entertainers and church leaders all wanting to get a firsthand look at conditions in the camps. Among them were Ted Kennedy, Mother Teresa, actors Charlton Heston and Cliff Robertson, and activist-comedian Dick Gregory, who staged a hunger strike in the coffee shop of the Addis Ababa Hilton in solidarity with the starving.

All of us who covered the famine came away with haunting memories.

For me, the most enduring was of a makeshift mortuary at Bati, a relief camp on the edge of the Danakil Desert that had sprung into existence only three weeks before and had a population of 25,000.

Laid out on the dirt floor of the mortuary—a circular structure made of wooden poles stuck into the ground and topped by a conical grass roof—were eight small bundles, wrapped in burlap sacking and stitched shut. They were the bodies of children who had died at Bati in the previous few hours.

As the late afternoon sun slanted through the gaps between the poles that formed the walls, two men were stitching together more burlap shrouds.

But words are not nearly as powerful as pictures—especially television footage.

"The world wakes up when we see images on the TV and when we see children dying," Jan Egeland, the United Nations' top aid official, told the BBC in the wake of its July reports on the famine in Niger.

"We have received more pledges in the past week than we have in six months. But it is too late for some of these children."

One parting note: Mohamed Amin, who more than anyone brought the Ethiopian famine to the world's attention, had just completed a visit to Addis Ababa on Nov. 23, 1996, when he boarded Ethiopian Airlines Flight 961 to return to Nairobi.

En route, the Boeing 767 was hijacked by a ragtag group of disgruntled Ethiopians who demanded that the plane be flown to Australia. As the airliner ran out of fuel near Comoros in the Indian Ocean, the pilot tried to ditch the plane in the reef-sheltered waters off Grand Comore. It broke up on the reef, killing 125 people, including Amin. He was 53.

The Problem with Predicting Famine

By Miren Gutierrez
Inter Press Service, May 3, 2006

Famines are almost a regular occurrence in many countries, especially in Africa, and recognizable signs of distress emerge well before people start to die. Why, then, is the response to food emergencies consistently slow?

"Predictability does make famines preventable so long as the countries have the means, know-how and the will to deal with the problem of food insecurity on a priority basis. In many cases, the countries or the donors may see other priorities for investments as more pressing," says a group of FAO experts in an e-mail interview*.

It seems preventability is too often not the priority.

"In general, early warnings by FAO/GIEWS (Global Information and Early Warning System) and other organizations like FEWS NET (Famine Early Warning Systems Network) alert the international community. Yet, having an effective early warning system is no guarantee that interventions will follow," add the FAO experts. "In some cases the response to these alerts is not immediate. Public response is galvanized when the stark images of hunger and destitute are shown on the television . . . the so-called 'CNN effect.'"

FEWS NET (part of the U.S. Agency for International Development, USAID) and its United Nations counterpart, the Food and Agriculture Organization's GIEWS, are the main alert agencies. The job of preventing hunger falls to World Food Program, another U.N. agency, and a number of private agencies. But funding their efforts is no one's responsibility in particular.

According to Anthea Webb, the WFP senior public affairs officer in Rome, "all information is available. The problem is to turn information into providing food to people in need. In Niger we had practically nothing until we got footage on video of people dying of malnutrition to the BBC. But it is much better to help people before it is too late. In Niger we had made a very clear plea. The problem is getting the message across."

To help do that, WFP initially set up a Web page called "Niger—A Chronology of Starvation."

After an abnormally short rainy season and a plague of locusts, at the end of 2004 WFP concluded that all the evidence indicated a food crisis was approaching: cereal prices had gone up, supplies were running low, people started eating seeds, the price of small livestock dropped as people sold those assets to buy food, the men left.

WFP publicized an urgent appeal for food on behalf of the government.

In May 2005, the U.N. country representative launched a "flash appeal" for Niger, seeking $16.1 million (which was increased to $18.3 million in June). A month later, only 11 percent of the requested funding had been received.

In July, the BBC broadcast footage gathered by WFP, showing children dying of malnutrition right before the cameras. A bit later, the U.N. renewed and increased its "flash appeal" to $30 million. Almost immediately, $10 million materialized.

To what point does the world's system for fighting mass hunger rely on media attention?

"We have warned for months about the problems in Mauritania and Mali, as with Niger, but the world can only cope with so much misery and the TV cameras' random gaze has yet to fall on these struggling nations. If one lesson was learned from Ethiopia's disastrous famine in the 1980s, it was that the world should listen to the early warnings and respond promptly," said WFP executive director James Morris, in an article published by *The Guardian* shortly after.

WFP received more donations for Niger in the last 10 days of June than it had in the previous eight months.

There are so many disasters happening in the world that for slow-growing catastrophes like the current ones in southern Africa or in the Horn of Africa, it is more difficult to seize media and donor attention.

Webb says that the regular promises of food aid pledged under the Food Aid Convention are being fulfilled without problems. But the aid needed to confront emergencies is another issue.

"Most years we get only around 80 percent (of the emergency aid required), but last year we even got less than that. Of course, we are very worried about the remaining 20 percent because it means that many have missed their meals, and afterwards it is too late to recuperate the loss of nutrients," she says in a telephone interview.

To what point does the world's system for fighting mass hunger rely on media attention?

"To the credit of many donors, well articulated and planned sustained effort is also practiced by many developed countries. . . . Obviously, spectacular disasters such as tsunami devastation in the Indian Ocean countries, the recent earthquake in Pakistan and subsequent misery due to bitter winter cold, malnourished children in

Niger, etc., have a tremendous effect on the public response," says FAO. "However, given the current levels of development assistance, much more needs to be done on this score."

"If it doesn't go on TV it is difficult to fund any effort," says the WFP's Webb. "But the situation last year was especially difficult: we had so many emergencies—the tsunami, Darfur, Niger, Pakistan— that it was a real trouble funding all. Many donors had exhausted their resources; there was a real donor fatigue. Let's hope 2006 is better."

To make up for the deficit, aid organizations are appealing to new donors and devising new ways of funding their operations.

"We are being more creative in the way we raise funds. Last year we raised $120 million from private individuals or companies—not much compared with the total $2.7 billion, but an important first step," says Webb. "We are also reaching non-traditional (donor) countries. We are now getting funds from India, Algeria, Malawi, Kenya, Libya, Russian Federation and China."

AXA Re, a commercial insurance company, was awarded the world's first insurance contract for humanitarian emergencies, WFP announced recently. The contract provides $7 million in contingency funding in a pilot scheme to provide coverage in the case of an extreme drought during Ethiopia's 2006 agricultural season.

> Early interventions are not only cheaper than tardy ones, they can also avoid some of the traps of food aid.

Other initiatives include a "humanitarian lottery," one drawing a year using any country's national lottery, whose proceeds would be donated to humanitarian efforts. "The lottery systems already exists; it would mean little to both the countries and the individuals," says Webb.

Early interventions are not only cheaper than tardy ones, they can also avoid some of the traps of food aid. Early intervention before people's livelihoods are ruined can offer cash or vouchers with which to buy food on the local market, rather than emergency rations to keep them alive.

During the World Trade Organization meeting in Hong Kong last December, European representatives blamed U.S. food aid for distortions in international farm trade and recipients' dependency on distribution of free food. The United States is the world's largest donor of food aid.

In a paper entitled "Food aid or hidden dumping?" Oxfam International, a confederation of anti-poverty organizations, argues that in-kind food aid can strengthen, not change, the status quo, while enriching U.S. grain companies.

"Agricultural exporting countries have called for new disciplines on food aid as part of the Doha Round negotiations at the WTO, in light of evidence that the USA sometimes uses food aid to dump agricultural surpluses and to attempt to create new markets for its exports," it reported.

"In recognition of such criticisms, the international community has actively sought in collaboration with host countries to make food aid respond only to verified demands and include more cash-based approaches," say the FAO experts. "FAO works with WFP through the approval process of its (Emergency Operations) to help avoid the potential negative effects on prices and farmers' incomes, generally through local purchases where possible."

In its Ethiopia report, FAO talks about a "new approach": cash aid instead of direct food aid. According to Oxfam, 90 percent of all food aid is provided in commodities rather than cash.

"FAO in general favors the 'twin track' approach, which refers to its emphasis on long-term development and capacity building in the crisis-prone countries, while at the same time providing immediate emergency assistance and safety net support to save lives and livelihoods," explains FAO.

Webb, however, says that direct food aid does not have such a negative impact.

According to her, WFP is "super careful" not to disturb local markets, calibrating quantities and choosing targets. "(Food aid) is directed to women, orphans, school-age children. . . . In 2005, we made 60 percent of our purchases in local markets.

"We feed people who are hungry, who don't have any purchasing power in any case, so the impact in the local markets is negligible," she says. Commercial production can hardly be hurt if there is no commercial production, Webb argues.

One would think that the old adage of "giving fishing rods instead of fish" would dominate the aid world by now, after so many deaths, such persistent death.

IV. WOMEN AND CHILDREN: GREATEST VICTIMS, GREATEST HOPE

Editor's Introduction

Worldwide, four out of every five people who die of hunger are women and children. Children in sub-Saharan Africa under five years of age die at 22 times the rate of children in industrialized nations and at twice the rate of the rest of the developing world, Michael Wines reports in the second article in this chapter. Women are also at a distinct disadvantage, as the cultures of many of the most hunger-stricken nations dictate that adult women are the last members of the family to eat—certainly after the men, but also after the elderly and the sick.

At the same time, women and children in developing nations are considered the countries' best chance to create an infrastructure that will eventually defeat hunger. With women composing 80 percent of the world's farmers, they play an important role in ensuring the steady production of food. "A green revolution will happen only if it is also a gender revolution," said former UN Secretary-General Kofi Annan, as quoted by Jan Goodwin in the first article of this chapter. Meanwhile, an increased emphasis on education points to the hope that the next generation will be better equipped to solve hunger in their home countries. This chapter explores the hardships women and children face in hunger-ravaged nations and the steps they are taking to empower themselves.

The famine in Niger is analyzed again in the first selection, "Do-It-Yourself Famine Fight" by Kirsten Scharnberg. In this look at Niger, however, Scharnberg focuses on the country's female population and the role of women in creating "sustainable solutions" to chronic hunger-the term relief agencies use for development programs, rather than simple food aid. Women, Scharnberg reports, are such a focus for these agencies because, unlike the men, who often leave the families to work in the cities, the women are always with their children; helping women, therefore, more directly helps the children as well.

In the next article, "Malnutrition Is Cheating Its Survivors, and Africa's Future," Wines reports on the nonfatal effects of malnutrition on children. While thousands of children die of starvation every year, thousands also survive, battling chronic hunger and its physical consequences, which can include stunted growth, diarrhea, and chronic coughs. Most distressingly, however, malnutrition often results in mental deficiencies, making rural education and development even more difficult. Governments and aid organizations hope to help by supplying nutritional supplements, such as salt iodization, fortification of flour, and semiannual doses of vitamins. Still, there is not sufficient aid to meet the level of need, and a whole generation has already felt the permanent effects of hunger.

Doctors in hunger-stricken regions attempt to battle these devastating effects, but many obstacles stand in the way of bringing sustained, quality medical care to children, as Anna Badkhen demonstrates in "Famine in East Africa." Badkhen writes from a treatment perspective, showing the frustrations of the doctors and hospital staff as they deal with the funding shortages and cultural pressures that often lead to incomplete treatment of their young patients.

In "Hunger Stalks Niger: The Rains and World Aid May Arrive Too Late to Save the Children," Scharnberg writes about Niger, this time focusing on the alarming rates of infant and child mortality. In Niger—a country where the mothers are sadly accustomed to the possibility of their child's death—even in years with good crops, 262 out of every 1,000 children die before the age of five, according to UNICEF. "It is the way of life that some babies die," one mother explains to Scharnberg.

Undernourishment alone causes massive suffering and numerous fatalities, especially in the particularly vulnerable age group of small children. But, as Carol Potera writes in the chapter's final article, "The Opposite of Obesity," undernourishment also makes children susceptible to infectious disease. Reporting the findings of a 2004 study, Potera presents data showing that even slight undernourishment greatly exacerbates the effects of infectious diseases in children, directly or indirectly causing half of all child deaths worldwide.

Do-It-Yourself Famine Fight

By Kirsten Scharnberg
Chicago Tribune, August 25, 2005

In their colorful dresses, holding children who cry from hunger, two dozen women gather beneath a twisted, ancient Tchedia tree. Sitting on the ground before them is a rusted metal box.

Baraka Sani pats the little box and explains how it changed her life three years ago.

"I bought a farm," the weathered 50-year-old said proudly. "I am the only woman in the village to own my own land."

The purchase was made possible by a loan from a cooperative credit union that was conceptualized by an international aid agency but now is run entirely by women in Sani's impoverished West African village. The credit union is rudimentary; money is stored in a shoebox-size metal container, and a sizable portion of revenue is generated by fining women who speak out of turn at bimonthly meetings of the credit union's 84 members.

Yet with her 1-acre plot, where she recently planted several rows of beans and peanuts, Sani represents the future of humanitarian aid in famine-stricken Niger, the perpetually underfed nation that UN Secretary General Kofi Annan visited Wednesday, vowing to use the power of the United Nations to "ensure what has happened this year does not happen in the future."

After visiting the remote region of Zinder, where he saw skeletal babies and listened to starving villagers plead for help, Annan seemed to concur with the assessment of many aid groups here—that simply handing out free food in Niger is not the answer.

"We will be looking forward to taking steps for the longer term to ensure food security," Annan said.

This is precisely the goal of many aid agencies that have been working in Niger, the second-poorest nation on Earth, since the famine hit critical levels earlier this year. Dozens of fix-it-yourself programs—intended to place the burden for preventing famines in the hands of the people—have been launched across the countryside, a clear shift in the aid approach to a nation that has become reliant on international assistance.

Crop Diversification Is Key

Humanitarian projects under way here attempt to teach people to diversify the crops they plant in order to introduce foods that provide more proteins and nutrients. They aim to stimulate the economy by adding a whole new segment of people with buying power: women. And they try to instill in the populace the importance of saving food and money so that during the years of drought or insect plagues there will be emergency reserves to draw on.

But for all the promise such successes as Sani's may hold, her foundering farm also illustrates the difficulty of effecting significant or speedy change in a deeply traditional, uneducated and impoverished land where people succumb to hunger in even the best of times and 262 out of every 1,000 children die before the age of 5.

For example, although Sani has heeded aid agencies' pleas to grow a few rows of alternate crops, the bulk of her land still is devoted to growing millet, the wheatlike, nutritionally poor food that the people of Niger have eaten for virtually every meal for generations. She was allowed to join the credit union and buy the land three years ago only after it was approved by her husband—who essentially considers the land his. And no matter how diligently she tills and

---

"The problem of hunger in Niger will not be solved easily."—Hassane Hamadou, CARE

---

hoes, Sani never can get far enough ahead to have adequate resources to draw on when famines strike, as they do about every four or five years.

"The problem of hunger in Niger will not be solved easily," said Hassane Hamadou of CARE, an international aid group active in Niger. "For centuries the famines have come. For centuries the people have starved. They know no other way. They accept this life."

As virtually everything does here, almost every aid agency's programs in some way revolve around millet, the crop that is the life force of Niger.

Millet is grown by almost all of the nation's 3.6 million farmers, but the crop has, ironically, become one of the very factors that work against the people of Niger, and in favor of malnutrition and hunger.

Day in and day out, women pound the grain to make meal for porridge and flour for pasta, and most diets consist almost solely of the grain. Still, the grain provides almost no protein or many other nutrients essential for the diets of growing children.

Aid agencies are trying hard to persuade farmers to diversify their incomes—and diets—by planting other crops and raising small animal herds. But such an attempt bucks tradition in Niger, where villages are known to shun families who begin growing other crops, dismissing the people as crazy. Farmers who try alternative crops tend to give up the experiment and revert to the familiar during years of crisis.

Shaibou Dankoulou, 65, was persuaded to grow peanuts on his small farm outside the village of Kalgo. The plants were thriving up until a few days ago, when Dankoulou's family became desperate for food. He sent his sons to the fields to pull up the entire crop nearly a month before it had fully matured, and the once-promising plants lay drying in the scorching sun.

"I had no choice," he said sadly. "We have nothing to eat. We are out of millet because of the drought and because we did not plant as much last year. So now we will sell all that we have pulled up to herders who need something to feed their cattle. That will make us a little money to buy food for now."

Dankoulou looked blankly at a visitor who asked what he would do in a few weeks, when the food he purchases is gone and there is no peanut crop to harvest for income for the coming year.

Calling Niger's hunger crisis complex is an understatement. But the first step in understanding it is knowing that even in the best of

---

Even in the best of years, most families can produce only enough millet to cover their food needs for about six or seven months of the year.

---

years, most families can produce only enough millet to cover their food needs for about six or seven months of the year. That frustrating fact is the result of many things: dry land that in many places is not well-suited to farming, lack of adequate farm tools, uncertain rains. In addition, Niger's population is growing at an alarming rate. Each woman bears an average of seven children, a trend that means the nation's underfed population is expected to double by 2026.

"There is no time to waste in teaching everything that we can to the people here," CARE's Hamadou said.

Children, gaunt and sick and too weak to lift their heads, are dying all over the country. There are no available estimates of how many have died this year—in the wake of a drought and locusts that decimated last year's crop—but Doctors Without Borders, the international relief agency, has treated nearly 15,000 starving children this year. Many could not be saved.

Aid groups are handing out food. But most of the focus is on "sustainable solutions" among Western aid workers who have descended on Maradi, the region where many of the groups are focusing their efforts.

Take, for example, a livestock-building initiative by UNICEF. The program began in one village in 1997 but has been greatly expanded recently.

The program works by giving five to seven male goats to a village. The program also gives to women with malnourished children two female goats, which are milked. The animals breed, producing up to four offspring a year. The women participating in the program must give the first two goats that are born to another local mother with malnourished children.

In the muddy little village of Safo, where the program began, Hadjia Haouaadamou's yard is chaotic with the bleats of six goats, four of which are pregnant.

The Haouaadamou family's entire millet crop was lost last year, but her goats have sustained them. The 51-year-old woman sold six goats about three months ago and used the proceeds to purchase food.

Aid agencies say Haouaadamou's story illustrates why they have spearheaded initiatives like the goat project, the women's-only credit union and women-run food banks that sell food at discounts to women with malnourished children.

Why the focus on women?

"The reason we focus so many of our programs on the women—and I think very many of the aid groups are doing the same thing—is that there is a direct advantage to the children when women are helped," said Chetima Moustapha, a native of Niger and assistant project coordinator for community development for UNICEF. "Women are always with the child, while sometimes men go off to work in the cities."

Even with her goats, Haouaadamou admits that the food store she purchased has run out. She is now—like so many in the nation—subsisting on leaves because she can not afford to buy millet and does not want to sell her remaining herd.

Only so much can be done to rush change in Niger.

In the village of Tessaoua, an old woman sat recently on the concrete floor of her one-room home and talked about all the famines she has seen. She said she is 135 years old, and whether that is true or not, she clearly believes she has struggled through a life that long.

Squinting at her visitors through cloudy eyes but drawing upon a memory that clearly has not faded with age, Rouba Badamassi said she could not begin to guess how much hunger she has known over the decades. She bore seven children; two starved to death. She remembers stealing grass from cattle to eat as a child and one particularly bad year in which people knocked apart termite hills and ant hills to take the wayward grains of millet the insects had stored there.

She knows aid groups are here to help and that they think the future of Niger could be different from its famished past. But Badamassi believes the will of man forever will be overshadowed by the will of God.

"Hunger is the phenomenon of God," the old woman said. "It is not man's responsibility but God's. God brings hunger. He will solve it. It is not the responsibility of man, and he should not pretend it is."

Malnutrition Is Cheating Its Survivors, and Africa's Future

By Michael Wines
The New York Times, December 28, 2006

In this corrugated land of mahogany mountains and tan, parched valleys, it is hard to tell which is the greater scandal: the thousands of children malnutrition kills, or the thousands more it allows to survive.

Malnutrition still kills here, though Ethiopia's infamous famines are in abeyance. In Wag Hamra alone, the northern area that includes Shimider, at least 10,000 children under age 5 died last year, thousands of them from malnutrition-related causes.

Yet almost half of Ethiopia's children are malnourished, and most do not die. Some suffer a different fate. Robbed of vital nutrients as children, they grow up stunted and sickly, weaklings in a land that still runs on manual labor. Some become intellectually stunted adults, shorn of as many as 15 I.Q. points, unable to learn or even to concentrate, inclined to drop out of school early.

There are many children like this in the villages around Shimider. Nearly 6 in 10 are stunted; 10-year-olds can fail to top an adult's belt buckle. They are frequently sick: diarrhea, chronic coughs and worse are standard for toddlers here. Most disquieting, teachers say, many of the 775 children at Shimider Primary are below-average pupils—often well below.

"They fall asleep," said Eteafraw Baro, a third-grade teacher at the school. "Their minds are slow, and they don't grasp what you teach them, and they're always behind in class."

Their hunger is neither a temporary inconvenience nor a quick death sentence. Rather, it is a chronic, lifelong, irreversible handicap that scuttles their futures and cripples Ethiopia's hopes to join the developed world.

"It is a barrier to improving our way of life," said Dr. Girma Akalu, perhaps the nation's leading nutrition expert. Ethiopia's problem is sub-Saharan Africa's curse. Five million African children under age 5 died last year—40 percent of deaths worldwide—and malnutrition was a major contributor to half of those deaths. Sub-Saharan children under 5 died not only at 22 times the rate of children in wealthy nations, but also at twice the rate for the entire developing world.

But below the Sahara, 33 million more children under 5 are living with malnutrition. In United Nations surveys from 1995 to 2003, nearly half of sub-Saharan children under 5 were stunted or wasted, markers of malnutrition and harbingers of physical and mental problems.

The world mostly mourns the dead, not the survivors. Intellectual stunting is seldom obvious until it is too late.

Bleak as that may sound, the outlook for malnourished children in sub-Saharan Africa is better than in decades, thanks to an awakening to the issue—by selected governments, anyway.

South Africa provides nutrient-fortified flour to 30 million of its 46 million citizens. Nigeria adds vitamin A to flour, cooking oil and sugar. Ethiopia's government hopes to iodize all salt by year's end. United Nations programs now cover three in four sub-Saharan children with twice-a-year doses of vitamin A supplements.

Ethiopia may, in fact, have the most comprehensive program in all Africa—a joint venture with United Nations agencies that regularly screens nearly half of its 14 million children under 5 for health and

---

The outlook for malnourished children in sub-Saharan Africa is better than in decades, thanks to an awakening to the issue.

---

nutrition problems. Since 2004, the program has delivered vitamin A doses and deworming medicine to 9 in 10 youngsters, vaccinated millions against childhood diseases and delivered fortified food and nutrition education.

Unicef's Ethiopia representative, Bjorn Ljungqvist, said the effort sprang from a disastrous 2003 drought in which global aid agencies fed 13.2 million Ethiopians—the most costly aid undertaking ever in Ethiopia. When the aid effort ended, he said, international donors and government officials decided that "we have to ensure that we don't get into this situation again."

The program may be a model for Africa: similar ones try to improve youngsters' health, but none, Dr. Ljungqvist said, addresses the nutritional deficiencies that leave children with life-long disabilities. The effort saves 100,000 lives a year, by Unicef estimates. And because it focuses not just on handouts, but on preventive care and nutrition education, the effects could be lasting.

Beyond that, as African nations develop Western-style mass markets, with brand names and national distribution networks, sales of vitamin-fortified foods are slowly becoming common in urban areas, just as in the West decades ago.

But much of the continent has far to go.

Well over half of sub-Saharan children under 5 lack iron, vital to developing nervous systems, the Micronutrient Initiative, a Canadian research organization, reported in 2004. They often have trouble concentrating and coordinating brain signals with movements, like holding a pencil, that are crucial to education.

Another 3.5 million children lack sufficient iodine, which can lower a child's I.Q. by 10 or more points. More than a half million suffer vitamin A deficiency, which cripples young immune systems; merely ensuring adequate vitamin A can lower child mortality by more than one-fifth. Children lacking vitamin B12, regularly measured nowhere in Africa, have impaired cognitive skills and do poorly on tests.

In most foods, these vital nutrients exist in traces—vitamins A and B12, iron, iodine, folic acid. Denied them in the womb and in infancy, children suffer irreversible brain and nervous-system damage, even if they appear well fed.

"Even trained people can't always see them," said Mark Fryars, the director of program services for the Micronutrient Initiative. "You may see a kid whose skin is very pale. You may go into a classroom where a child wanders off, or falls asleep, or doesn't go out to play because he's too tired. Multiply that into whole villages, and that translates into an impact on the society."

In richer parts of the world, nutritional deficiencies are a nonissue. Three percent of American children are malnourished. American flour and cereals have been fortified with vitamins and iron—by law—since the 1930s.

In sub-Saharan Africa, however, lost productivity from vitamin and mineral deficiencies costs nations $2.3 billion a year, Unicef reports, and losses of productivity in Mozambique, Zambia and Malawi exceeded 1 percent of gross domestic product.

Many African children sometimes receive nutrient supplements, courtesy of the World Food Program, Unicef and charities. Still, donors cannot meet the need. In Ethiopia, for example, a venture between the government and United Nations agencies is caring for 20,000 acutely malnourished children at 100 sites.

"But we can count 70,000," said Iqbal Kabir, the chief nutrition expert at Unicef offices in Addis Ababa, Ethiopia's capital. "We can't treat them all."

Shimider is but a hundred or so stone and reed homes, one room each, in a mountain valley in the Amhara region, 250 miles north of Addis Ababa. The slopes here have been intensively farmed for thousands of years, and their soils are exhausted.

Twenty-two years ago, a famine here killed more than one million people. Today, hunger is measured in squandered lives.

Thirty percent of Amhara's children under 5 are stunted, with another 26 percent severely stunted, evidence of lifelong, acute hunger. One in 15 pregnant women experiences night blindness, indicating vitamin A deficiency and a diet devoid of protein and red or yellow fruits and vegetables.

Among both malnourished children and their mothers, the impact of such privation is achingly evident.

One recent Sunday, Tewres Beram, a woman in her early 20s, carried her daughter Mekdes to a free immunization clinic. Mekdes, severely malnourished, sat suckling fruitlessly at her mother's breast. "We don't have enough food," her mother said, "so there's not enough milk to feed her." A year old, Mekdes does not crawl. Her sister, 2, has barely begun to crawl. "Both of them are like little dead bodies," their mother said.

Sirkalem Birhanu, 40, clasps Endalew, age 2 and unable even to hold up his head. "He's always sick," she said. Endalew has company, she said; his 13-year-old brother "is very tiny, and he loses weight."

"And he's always been sick," she added.

And there is Berhane Gebeyew, 36, whose malnourished 18-month-old daughter, Genet, is a lump in her lap, despite receiving six months' worth of fortified food last May from the governments.

> Virtually all nutritional deficiencies can be easily and cheaply prevented, sometimes for pennies per child.

Mrs. Gebeyew split the food among Genet and her four siblings, ages 6 to 15. "The other children, when they stare at my eyes, I give it to them," she said.

She and her husband feed their children two daily meals of injera, a spongy flatbread of fermented barley, occasionally with four ounces of bean sauce. When the children attend Shimider Primary, each gets 10 ounces of vitamin-fortified meal mixed with cooking oil. But attendance is spotty, especially when they help harvest crops in November and December.

And by the time children reach school age, much of malnutrition's damage has already been wrought.

Wondewosen Fekadu is the headmaster at Shimider Primary. Mr. Fekadu worked last year in Tseta, a lowland village where families eat better and drink milk. The difference in their students, he said, is striking. "Children there are relatively smarter and more active," he said. "There are students here who are up to fourth grade and they cannot even read and write, even attentively following the classes."

Three of Mrs. Gebeyew's children attend Shimider Primary. Mogus, a 10-year-old third grader, is three and one-half feet tall—wide-eyed, sweet and flummoxed by academics.

"He's on the poor level—very slow," his teacher said. "He doesn't give attention when I'm teaching. He doesn't concentrate." In a classroom of 60 children, Mogus ranks 46th.

Mulu, 13, her ribs prominent through rips in her green school dress, races from home to get to her beloved third-grade class. But Mulu is 47th in a class of 60.

Fifteen-year-old Yirgalem, about two inches taller than Mulu, has a teenager's diffidence toward school. "It's not that tough," he said. His second-grade teachers differ. "When he comes to school, I don't even think his mind is normal," one of his teachers, Amelework Ejigu, said.

There is great promise that this region's future youngsters will not be hobbled by mental disabilities. Virtually all nutritional deficiencies can be easily and cheaply prevented, sometimes for pennies per child, through programs like universal salt iodization, fortification of flour and semiannual doses of vitamins.

Such efforts already are under way in some nations, and they are a foundation of most United Nations children's programs. But in just as many places, they remain a promise.

At Tefera Hailu Memorial Hospital in Sekota, across a mountain from Shimider, the nutrition ward's 10 beds are filled with worried mothers and shrunken babies. Among them are Adna Berhanu and her 5-month-old son, Agnecheu.

Mrs. Berhanu's huge goiter is decorated with blue tribal tattoos. Her skeletal baby is severely iodine deficient, surely impaired for life should he survive.

Although iodine deficiency is endemic in Amhara Province, "I've been here a year, and we have no iodine in this ward," the nurse on duty said. Beyond a blood test to estimate iron content, the attending physician said, no one even analyzes children's nutritional status. Such tests, he said, are luxuries.

"We focus on saving lives; that's our long-term focus," he said. "We can't focus on what happens to them afterward."

Famine in East Africa

Littlest Victims of Drought, Poverty

By Anna Badkhen
The San Francisco Chronicle, March 30, 2006

Over the buzz of hospital ceiling fans, Habiba Mohammed heard the slightest murmur emerge from her daughter's wasted chest: The baby was hungry. She pulled down the top of her dress and offered her emaciated child a breast that had not had milk for months.

Her daughter, Hadiwa, is a casualty of a sustained, four-year drought that is threatening the lives of 17 million people across East Africa. Her ankles are no thicker than an adult's thumb; wrinkled skin hangs loosely around her thighs and angular pelvic bones. She is 9 months old and weighs 8 pounds, just over a pound more than her birth weight. Tuberculosis, malaria and pneumonia are eating away at her tiny body.

She could recover, say doctors at Garissa [Kenya] Provincial Hospital, but it will take at least two months of intensive feeding. Mohammed, 19, says she cannot wait that long.

"There are things I need to attend to at home," she said, her eyes fixed on the tiled hospital floor.

After the drought destroyed the pastures and killed off the family's livestock, her husband was forced to go to Garissa to look for work as a day laborer. Now their house of sticks and straw, in the dry bush several miles south of Garissa, remains unattended. If she does not return home soon, someone might steal their sleeping mats and cooking utensils—and maybe even the house itself, Mohammed said.

It's a cruel dilemma that doctors at the Garissa hospital see repeatedly.

Their families living in abject poverty, children on the brink of starvation who are brought to the Garissa hospital rarely complete their treatment because of social and economic pressures on their mothers, said Dr. Khadija Abdalla, the chief pediatrician at the hospital.

"Often they have to return to their other children, whom they've left in the bush. Sometimes they come with other children, which puts these new children at risk of contracting disease. Husbands also pressurize them to return," said Abdalla. "It's very frustrating, especially when you know that they're going to have to come back."

At least 500,000 Kenyan children face the threat of starvation as the worst drought to hit East Africa in decades enters its fourth year, aid agencies say, and cases of severe malnutrition are on the rise. The drought and subsequent famine stretch across swaths of Kenya, Ethiopia, Eritrea, Somalia, Djibouti and Sudan, countries that are simply not prepared to deal with the looming humanitarian crisis, say international aid officials.

The Garissa hospital is the only medical facility that provides therapeutic feeding to children in Kenya's drought-ravaged North Eastern province of 400,000 people. Twenty children diagnosed with severe malnutrition are currently receiving treatment, 10 times the usual number, said Abdalla. Since December, seven children admitted to the hospital have died.

The real number of children suffering and dying without being seen by doctors is probably much higher, she said.

As it is, the hospital is barely able to cope with the number of patients it has. The pediatric ward, meant to treat a maximum of 50 children, had 56 patients Monday. As the effects of the famine

---

> At least 500,000 Kenyan children face the threat of starvation as the worst drought to hit East Africa in decades enters its fourth year.

---

intensify, those numbers, too, are likely to increase dramatically, say medical workers. The nurses—just two per shift—can do little more than weigh the children and deliver medicine. This means mothers must stay with their sick children day and night. But many of these mothers—some of whom have just reached adolescence themselves—don't make the best caregivers, Abdalla said.

"Most mothers are illiterate. You can't instruct them," she said. "Sometimes the children get four or five (therapeutic) feeds a day instead of the nine that are required."

Many mothers don't have the money to pay for their children's treatment, like Ladhah Abdulla, 20, the mother of Malyun Osman, a skeletal 2-year-old girl weighing 12.7 pounds.

Her husband left for South Africa two years ago when Abdulla was still pregnant with Malyun. The husband said he would look for work there and send money home, but so far, no money and no word have come from him. Abdulla, who also has a 5-year-old son, Faisul, moved in with her parents, impoverished herders who themselves barely have the means to get by.

So far, the hospital has waived the costs of Malyun's treatment— the equivalent of 70 cents per day. But Abdulla does not know how long this benevolence will last. Doctors say Malyun, who spends her days playing with breadcrumbs in a beat-up aluminum bowl on her cot by a window covered with anti-mosquito netting, will need six months to recover.

"I'm not sure how long I will stay here," Abdulla said. "I can't afford to pay for the bed."

Four cots away, Batula Guhat faced a similar situation. Two weeks ago, after a 100-mile walk through the bush that took almost two months, Guhat, 53, brought her bird-like granddaughter, Fatuma Hillow, 2, to the hospital. Fatuma weighs less than 10 pounds; her hands are so small that doctors have to inject her anti-tuberculosis medications into her feet. Fatuma's chest protrudes abnormally; last week, her heart stopped temporarily.

After 10 days at the hospital, doctors realized that she needed to go to the capital, Nairobi, to see a cardiologist the Garissa hospital doesn't have.

"The problem is, if you give them an alternative to go to Nairobi, they opt not to because they can't afford it," Abdalla said before she gave Guhat the news.

Guhat considered her options. The hospital would pay for the transportation to Nairobi, but there will be expensive tests and even more expensive treatment, possibly surgery.

"I can't afford to go," Guhat said.

A minute later, Abdalla learned that her other patient, little Hadiwa, also will not receive the full treatment she needs.

"She will gain one more kilo," (2.2 pounds), "and then we'll leave," said Hadiwa's mother as she avoided the doctor's eyes. Seven other mothers, who were listening in the hospital room, where the temperature was above 100 degrees, kept fanning their emaciated children with the loose ends of their colorful scarves. Abdalla lifted her eyebrows and pursed her lips. She knew she could not stop Mohammed from leaving any more than she could make it rain and break the devastating drought.

So all she said, as her gaze rested on a banana peel on a wooden stool near Hadiwa's cot, was: "You've made this place a mess. It's unsanitary. You have to keep it clean."

Hunger Stalks Niger

BY KIRSTEN SCHARNBERG
CHICAGO TRIBUNE, AUGUST 10, 2005

Balancing a 100-pound bag of grain on top of her head, Koini Ousala trudged uphill to her corner of this remote village of one-room mud huts.

She had much to do, Ousala explained. She had to pound her sack of millet into meal for porridge and flour for pasta. She had to fairly divide the food—provided by an American humanitarian aid group and not likely to last quite two weeks—among the more than three dozen members of her family. And she had to try to coax several of the children, including a granddaughter who at the age of 2 is nearly as small as a 5-month-old cousin, into eating, a difficult task because the youngsters are so malnourished that their stomachs no longer can hold most food.

"Six of my family's babies have already died," Ousala said without pause. "Go have a look at the graves. See for yourself. I will stay here and work."

Life is never easy and food is never abundant in Niger, the second-poorest nation on Earth. But after being hit last year by a drought that killed most crops and a plague of locusts that devoured anything remaining after that, this vast African nation that perpetually teeters on the brink of a hunger crisis has plunged into full-fledged famine.

Women like Ousala, a practical matriarch who looks puzzled when asked whether all the death makes her bitter or angry, don't have time to mourn the children who die because others, just as emaciated and just as ill, follow behind them.

Over the past several months, medical clinics to treat the thousands of children and infants suffering from starvation have sprung up in Niger's larger cities. Experts have come to teach better agricultural practices to the nearly 3.6 million farmers whose millet supports the diet of almost every citizen. And food banks have begun distributing free food—though it has taken so long to get supplies to such places as Douloukou, a village accessible only by a three-hour, bone-shattering drive down a mud road, that for many families there is no way to turn back the clock.

Hunger Nothing New

Though the cameras and the attention have focused on Niger this year, hunger—even hunger that reaches deadly and epidemic proportions—is not new here. In even the years of good rains and bumper crops, 262 out of every 1,000 children in Niger die before age 5, UNICEF says.

But the famines, like this summer's, propel the tragedy to new levels. Although no figures exist for how many people have died of hunger this year in Niger, the United Nations has estimated that 874,000 urgently need food.

In much the same way that Midwesterners remember particularly hard winters, Niger's citizens mark time by the severity of certain years' food crises and the number of children who died. There is a national expression that "years that end in 4 are always bad," referring to numerous terrible famines—particularly the one that followed the miserable harvest of 1984—that have so badly ravaged this nation since as long as anyone can remember.

> In even the years of good rains and bumper crops, 262 out of every 1,000 children in Niger die before age 5, UNICEF says.

"In even the years of greatest crop production, the poorest people—which is about 60 percent of the country—have only enough food to cover six or seven months of their needs," said Hassane Hamadou, the director of the Niger office for CARE, an international humanitarian aid group that has been working in Africa for decades.

"In the bad years—when there is not enough rain, when there are locusts, when the land does not produce—they have only enough to cover about three months."

Hamadou's assessment means that after a year as disastrous as 2004, most people in Niger ran out of food sometime in January, three months after the harvest that usually ends in October. His prediction seems to be borne out in the far-flung villages, where children have long since begun to die, where the carcasses of starved cattle litter the countryside, where the sense of fatalism is so pronounced that women—like a young mother in Douloukou who sobbed in panic when she bore twins this week—solemnly expect they will lose at least one of their children to the hunger.

"It is the way of life that some babies die," said Aishata Yaou, the mother of Mansour, a 4-year-old so weak from hunger Tuesday that he could not lift his head. With a force that shook his tiny body from the top of a head balding because of lack of nutrients to toes with malformed nails, he vomited any food or water he consumed within minutes.

Niger is among Africa's largest nations, a behemoth almost twice the size of Texas. Most of the population lives in the southern part of the nation, below the Sahara, where they can grow millet, a wheat-like crop that thrives only if enough rain falls in August, the traditional but often unreliable rainy season.

Driving through the villages of southern Niger, one can see, even architecturally, how central millet is to life here. Every family has a round, thatched-roof granary near their home where millet is stored between harvests. In theory, a family's stockpile would last the entire year, and they would use it for everything: daily meals, a form of currency, dowries and payment for social events such as baby-naming ceremonies or weddings.

Granaries in Disrepair

But this year, almost every family's granary is empty. The roofs have blown off, and no one has put them back on; there is nothing inside that needs protection from the rain anyway. And although families usually put more priority on maintaining the granary than their home, many of the granaries have collapsed, a series of broken structures that perfectly illustrate the collapse of the food stores here.

As early as last year, agriculture experts warned that the already-impoverished nation of 11.7 million people had produced just 7.5 percent of its typical crop in the aftermath of the drought and locust plague. That translated to a nearly 220,000-ton shortage of millet.

Knowing that millet is served daily in some form—soaked in water to make a sort of cloudy "milk" for breakfast, in a porridge for lunch and as pasta in the evenings—aid groups such as the UN World Food Program and Doctors Without Borders loudly predicted a crisis. The Niger government put out a call late last year for 71,000 tons of food aid and $3 million to help farmers. It got just 7,000 tons of food and well less than a half-million dollars, government and World Food Program officials say.

The millet shortage is visible not only on the exposed ribs of the children dying in places like Douloukou or inside the sprawling Doctors Without Borders health clinic in the city of Maradi, where some 300 severely malnourished children and their mothers huddle in dank tents while they are given medical treatment. It also is noticeable in most village markets. Where once every other stand would have traded in millet, now many stands are instead selling leaves pulled from trees. The people mix them with water and spices to eat.

Perhaps most worrisome is that experts predict the situation is only going to deteriorate. No one knows yet how this year's millet crop will fare—the rains of August will determine that—but the harvest is at least two months away.

Even more, the rain may help the millet, but it also brings mosquitoes and the resulting malaria. Babies already weak from hunger are unable to stave off the disease.

"I'm afraid we are about to see things get much worse," said Dr. Vanessa Remy-Piccolo, a French physician who works with Doctors Without Borders, a group that has treated more than 14,000 severely malnourished children in Niger this year, more than double the number treated in 2004.

Remy-Piccolo on Tuesday saw tiny Halima Moussa, a gaunt 4-year-old girl who was just 14 1/2 pounds when she arrived at the clinic in Maradi on Monday night. Her arms and legs were like twigs; she could not stand, could barely open her eyes. She did not have the energy to cry when the nurses poked her finger to do a malaria blood test. Her eyes showed fright, but she did not utter a sound, did not even gasp, as if the intake of air would require too much strength.

Halima's mother, Indo, knows about famine and death. She does not know her age but guessed she was around 40. Of her 14 children, 10 have died, most from starvation.

Last year, Indo had brought her two youngest remaining children, Halima and her little brother, to the same clinic in Maradi. The boy died. Halima survived, only to see another famine.

"It's All God's Will"

In a tent crowded with dozens of other mothers and children Tuesday, Indo cradled an unresponsive Halima. The mother looked at her child and said, quite practically: "Some live. Some die. It's all God's will. Even hunger is God's will."

On Monday night, even as doctors were admitting Halima into the Maradi clinic, the skies of the region opened up to deliver one of the first big rains of August, the month said to make or break every year's millet crop. Young children joyfully ran up and down the mud roads, splashing in the puddles. Women smiled even as the rain soaked their brightly colored clothes.

"All hope is on the millet," said Moussa Harouna. "We work hard, and maybe this year it will be better."

The rain also fell in Douloukou, where Koini Ousala prepared her first meal with the millet she had received that morning at the CARE distribution site, the first to serve people so remotely located in the Dakoro region. She offered a visitor a plate, even though she knew that the sack would run out well before any harvest could be reaped.

Several hundred yards away, under an African Kamatche tree, one small patch of valuable land lay unfarmed. It is the family's burial ground, and the earth there holds more babies and children than old men and women. The little cemetery is surrounded by millet fields.

The Opposite of Obesity

Undernutrition Overwhelms the World's Children

By Carol Potera
Environmental Health Perspectives, October 2004

An alarming number of studies report that overnutrition and the resulting obesity are a growing health problem for children in industrialized nations and even some developing ones. The explosion of such studies might seem to suggest that starvation is a thing of the past, yet children in many developing countries still go hungry. Furthermore, a lack of calories and nutrients—or undernutrition—can worsen the effects of infectious disease, and thereby causes half of all child deaths worldwide, report public health experts at The Johns Hopkins University and the World Health Organization in the 1 July 2004 issue of the *American Journal of Clinical Nutrition*.

This new finding supports a 1995 study coordinated by David Pelletier, an associate professor of nutrition sciences at Cornell University, which provided the first evidence of how often child deaths are attributable to undernutrition. The latest study goes a step further: Johns Hopkins nutritionist Laura Caulfield and her colleagues answer the important question of whether undernutrition exacerbates the effects of infectious diseases.

Caulfield headed a team that analyzed data from 10 large studies of child deaths in sub-Saharan Africa and Southeast Asia. These studies included data about the average weight-for-age status of children relative to healthy U.S. reference children. Unlike Pelletier's work, the studies reviewed by Caulfield's team contained information about the cause of death, allowing the team to tease out the role of undernutrition in deaths caused by diarrhea, malaria, measles, and pneumonia.

Weight-for-age is the most widely used indicator of child nutritional status in developing countries. Caulfield's team compared the weight-for-age of children relative to the "international growth reference" established by the National Center for Health Statistics. Children who fall below –2 standard deviations are classified as moderately to severely undernourished (in developing countries, 30–50% of children fall into this category). The team then used a statistical model to relate weight-for-age scores to the death rate.

Overall, the team found having a low weight-for-age score is a leading risk factor for child deaths, accounting for 52.5% worldwide. Among individual diseases studied, undernutrition is responsible for 60.7% of deaths from diarrhea, 57.3% of deaths from malaria, 52.3% of deaths from pneumonia, and 44.8% of deaths from measles.

Moreover, children do not need to be severely undernourished to be at heightened risk of dying if an infectious disease strikes. "Our analysis shows that even children who are small [for their age], but who would not be classified as malnourished based on their weight, are twice as likely to die as children of normal weight," says Caulfield. "Undernutrition increases the susceptibility to illness and increases the likelihood that an illness will be severe."

Before Caulfield's study and the earlier one by Pelletier, experts estimated that undernutrition accounted for no more than 5% of child deaths; cause of death was attributed only to obvious disease symptoms, such as diarrhea or fever. These earlier estimates "did

---

Children do not need to be severely undernourished to be at heightened risk of dying if an infectious disease strikes.

---

not capture the underlying effect of malnutrition in making a disease more severe," says Pelletier, who calls undernutrition "the silent killer."

Public health experts and policy makers historically look to immunizations, drug treatments, and sanitation as ways to prevent child deaths. Programs such as the Millenium Development Goals of the United Nations (which promises to cut the mortality rate of children under age 5 by two-thirds by the year 2015) and vaccination accessibility and research projects funded by the Bill & Melinda Gates Foundation suggest that the international community is committed to improving child health through such means.

But disease treatment and prevention are not enough, says Pelletier; money must also go toward educational and agricultural programs to abate undernutrition. "The impact of undernutrition is not as well appreciated," agrees Caulfield. Her findings emphasize the need to invest in nutrition programs globally to reduce child deaths.

The new findings are a wake-up call to policy makers about the implications of undernutrition. "The data are there," says Caulfield, "but we need to translate them for policy makers so that they can understand what it means for a child to weigh less than normal." In addition to preventing child deaths, correcting undernutrition contributes to quality of life. Even if antibiotics and immunizations keep children alive, "their quality of life is miserable if they're malnourished," says Pelletier.

V. PROMISING SOLUTION OR RISKY EXPERIMENT? THE BIOTECHNOLOGY DEBATE

Editor's Introduction

The "Green Revolution" movement of the 1950s and 1960s brought new agricultural technology—such as chemical fertilizers and pesticides, irrigation projects, and "high-yield" crop varieties—to the developing world. This influx of information and technology spurred huge changes throughout Asia and likely prevented a great famine on the continent. But this farming revolution—a costly endeavor developed for temperate zone agriculture—never made it to Africa. Now the world is in the midst of the "Gene Revolution." Led largely by U.S. corporations, the "Gene Revolution" seeks to employ biotechnology and genetically modified (GM) crops to fight world hunger, specifically in Africa. But while the American government heralds the advantages of GM produce, the rest of the world—especially the European Union—remains ambivalent. This chapter presents both sides of the debate over using GM crops to alleviate world hunger.

In "So Shall We Reap," the first piece in this chapter, Peter Pringle looks at the situation in Zambia, which, in 2002, refused to accept food aid in the form of GM produce. Using Zambia's decision as a focal point, Pringle discusses the larger question of biotechnology's role in Africa. The political "war" that is being played out in Africa between the United States and the European Union over the morality and science of biotechnology has obscured the practicalities of the situation, Pringle asserts. Given the state of their agricultural practices, he says, developing nations are not yet in a position to even consider growing transgenic crops. Indeed, the hugely expensive costs associated with GM agriculture prevent even small American farmers from entering the field. Instead of engaging in this counterproductive debate, Pringle writes, industrialized nations ought to work collectively to help developing nations modernize their farming practices.

Frustrated and starving, one group of Zambians took matters into their own hands, raiding a government warehouse where GM grain from the United States was sequestered. In "Debate Grows Over Biotech Food," Justin Gillis uses this incident to explore the viability of biotechnology in Africa, asking whether the average African citizen wants the option of planting GM crops. Ultimately, he concludes, Africans seem to welcome the technology overall, but he argues that what they really need is more infrastructure, in the form of crop storage facilities, better roads, an improved farm-credit system, and better access to agricultural supplies.

In "Genetic Engineering Is Not the Answer," Sean McDonagh makes a similar argument, pointing to the absence of land reform, social inequality, and the lack of affordable credit and basic agricultural tools as the main factors in world hunger. Even were these problems to be fixed, however, McDonagh remains leery of GM crops. One of his chief concerns is the question of ownership. The corporations that develop these crops want to patent them, leading to a number of moral implications and large economic consequences.

The final article in this chapter is an editorial from *USA Today*, "Feed Starving Masses, Not Irrational Fears." While acknowledging the risks inherent in biotechnology, the authors argue that the immediate necessity of feeding the world's hungry outweighs the hypothetical dangers of GM crops. The writers call on Europe to relax its own standards, alleviating pressure on African nations to also resist GM crops.

So Shall We Reap

From *Food, Inc.*

BY PETER PRINGLE
SIMON & SCHUSTER, 2003

> One thing is sure: the earth is more cultivated and developed
> now than ever before; there is more farming but fewer forests,
> swamps are drying up and cities are springing up on an
> unprecedented scale. We have become a burden to our planet.
> Resources are becoming scarce and soon nature will no longer be
> able to satisfy our needs
>
> —QUINTUS SEPTIMUS TERTULLIANUS, 200 B.C.

Across southern Africa in 2002 the harvests failed, leaving almost
15 million people facing starvation. Drought one month, floods the
next destroyed crops across the continent, but AIDS and local political turmoil had also exacted their toll. As boreholes went dry and
crops withered, the world saw the all-too-familiar pictures of women
and children lining up for their daily handful of grain or flour
offered by nations with plenty. The African famine of 2002 had a
new dimension, however. Three countries—Zimbabwe, Mozambique, and Zambia—made the astonishing decision to refuse food
from the United States containing genetically modified seeds. Fear
of the new seeds was so great that leaders—presumably well-fed
leaders—decided to chance their luck and look elsewhere for help.

How did the fear of GM foods rise to this tragic level? A decade
after Americans had eaten their first GM food—a harmless tomato
that ripened more slowly—farmers had planted genetically modified
seed on more than 130 million acres worldwide. But biotech companies had failed to convince the international community outside the
United States—even nations in Africa on the brink of starvation—
that these novel crops were safe for humans and the environment.

Under pressure from UN relief agencies, Zimbabwe and Mozambique agreed to take the U.S. corn, providing it was milled and free
of seeds that might be planted. The Zambian government stub-
bornly refused the aid altogether. "Simply because my people are
hungry, is not a justification to give them poison," declared Zambia's
president, Levy Mwanawasa.

From the American perspective, the Zambian decision looked churlish and irresponsible. A small, undeveloped nation of 10 million with traditional agricultural methods, poor soils, and an inhospitable climate was putting nearly 3 million people at risk of starvation by turning away food. Moreover, this food was being offered by the world's most powerful industrialized nation, a country with the most technologically advanced agricultural system and the most safety-conscious consumers.

The U.S. corn that might have gone to Zambia, or any other nation, unavoidably contained genetically modified grains. One-third of the corn planted in the United States is genetically modified, and because it is not separated in the American grain system, American food aid corn is not guaranteed to be GM-free. In 2001 the UN's World Food Program, which distributes aid donated by individual countries, fed these GM foods to 52 million people.[1] The United States offered unmodified wheat or rice, but the Zambians only wanted corn.

From an African perspective, however, the Zambian decision looked quite different. First, the Zambian government did not believe that it had made an irresponsible decision. There was no question of letting its citizens die of starvation. There was plenty of non-GM corn in the world's granaries and the Zambians believed they would be able to secure enough of it with donated aid funds from elsewhere. Second, Zambia was not against GM crops per se, but the government had been advised by its top scientists to favor the precautionary principle—which basically meant that until a food was proved safe, it was off-limits. The Zambian scientists had come to this conclusion after seeking advice from experts on both sides of the debate in Europe, the United States, and South Africa. The scientific group had concluded that GM food was still a potential health hazard and, citing the recent Mexican gene flow example, that American corn could contaminate local African varieties. Among the familiar health concerns cited by the Zambians were that GM foods could produce unpredictable toxins or new allergens and that antibiotic-resistant marker genes were still being used in America and could potentially cause harm. In addition, the Zambian scientists noted that while millions of Americans may consume corn in processed foods such as cornflakes and taco chips, Zambians do not eat corn as a staple food. In Zambia, unprocessed corn is the staple food and usually the only source of carbohydrate.

A third reason for rejecting the U.S. aid was that Zambia, like other African countries, exports agricultural products to Europe and European consumers were basically anti-GM. Until now, Zambia had remained GM-free and the government was concerned that if it allowed the U.S. corn into the country that their farmers would be tempted to plant the new seeds as well as eat them. The country's corn crop would then be contaminated in European eyes, and Zambian exports might suffer—even though the exports were mainly horticultural and did not include corn.

The fourth reason was that Zambia, again like most African nations, still lacked a system of internal regulations for monitoring and testing GM crops and products. For several years, the developing countries had sought a way of regulating the import and cultivation of GM crops and foods. In 2000 they had succeeded, against U.S. opposition, in securing an amendment known as the Biosafety Protocol to the 1993 Convention on Biological Diversity (CBD). This amendment gave governments the right to regulate GM foods.[2] The protocol required exporters of GM seeds for planting to give the importing country written notification of their arrival. Yet, there was no such obligation for crops used in processed foods or for grains intended for direct human or animal consumption. Thus, the United States had no obligation to notify the Zambians, or any other country, that they were sending food aid that may contain GM corn. Indeed, the U.S. had been sending such corn as food aid for several years.[3]

The incident quickly escalated into a full-blown diplomatic row. America accused the cautious Europeans of persuading the Africans that genetically modified foods might be unsafe. In turn the Europeans suggested that the Americans were cynically trying to shove corn they could not sell elsewhere down the throats of starving Africans, and calling it charity. EU officials went to Zambia to explain that if Zambia grew GM corn, it would not affect the country's ability to export other agricultural products—vegetables, flowers, and coffee. Those products would be unaffected because they don't mate with corn.

The U.S. Secretary of Agriculture, Ann Veneman, blamed antibiotech forces for scaring Zambians into believing that GM corn would harm them. "It is disgraceful that instead of helping hungry people, these individuals and organizations are embarking on an irresponsible campaign to spread misinformation and create an atmosphere of fear, which has led countries in dire need of food to turn away safe, wholesome food."[4] While Veneman's target appeared to be such staunch biotech opponents as Greenpeace and Friends of the Earth, the United States was also threatening to declare a trade war on Europe for its four-year moratorium on the approval of new GM products. The ban was hurting American farmers; the American government was expected to appeal to the World Trade Organization, charging protectionism.

Longtime antibiotech campaigners were quick to pick up on the cynical view of the U.S. aid. Hope Shand, of the antibiotech ETC Group (the Action Group on Erosion, Technology, and Concentration), formerly RAFI, said, "The U.S. and the biotechnology industry have been desperate to show the benefits of this technology. Now they are trying to sell the product by giving it away."[5] The science journal *Nature* picked up on another aspect of the U.S. donation. U.S. food aid grants and loans are only available for the procurement of grain from U.S. farmers. The journal noted sarcastically the "extent to which aid donors like to enjoy most of the fruits of their own benevolence"; American farmers would be receiving "a few dollars more on top of the billions being lavished on domestic farm support."[6]

In many ways the biotech industry and the U.S. government had only themselves to blame for this latest fiasco. Since the beginning, while the industry claimed that their products would save the world from malnutrition, seed companies created only crops that made money for themselves and the wealthier farmers who could afford the premiums. Even Western consumers were yet to receive a direct benefit from these novel foods.

Bound by its "substantially equivalent" doctrine—which declared the new foods safe because they were substantially equivalent to the old ones—the U.S. government had told consumers that a transgenic tomato was just like an ordinary tomato, even though bioengineers acknowledged that there were substantial differences. Ignoring the distinctions, the U.S. government and the grain merchants had not required farmers to separate their harvest into GM and non-GM grains, so when it came to offering starving nations food aid, there was essentially no choice. Zambia's decision polarized the debate, leaving both sides looking as though they had bungled the affair. As the Zambian agricultural minister, Guy Scott, told *Time* magazine, "I don't think there are any particular heroes or villains in this whole thing, it's just a balls-up."[7]

In the brief, turbulent history of biotech agriculture, the Zambian famine also turned into another bitter contest for public opinion. This time, however, millions of people were on the brink of starvation while the two sides engaged in yet another war of words. Once again, a quest for the scientific truth of GM foods was undermined by special interests. The debate became the most poignant in a long list of events that had eroded public confidence in the new crops— golden rice, the cornfields of Oaxaca, potatoes with snowdrop genes, the monarch butterfly, patents on basmati rice and yellow Mexican beans, StarLink corn, and the mysterious escape of canola genes on Percy Schmeiser's farm in Saskatchewan. The Zambian incident also refocused attention on the developing world as the new front line in the biotech wars.

In North America, the birthplace of biotech, the revolution was stalled by 2003. Farmers could not sell GM crops in several international markets and were reluctant to consider new biotech products. In America 35 percent of the corn crop and 75 percent of the soybean crop was GM, but worldwide, the figures dropped dramatically—to 36 percent of soybeans, and 7 percent of corn. The European market remained bleak. Consumer opposition was still high; the EU was about to introduce strict labeling rules for GM foods. The outcome of the British farm-scale trials of GM crops—the most comprehensive tests so far of the effects of these crops on the environment—was expected in the summer of 2003. Even governments, such as Japan's, that had allowed GM imports slowed their approval after the StarLink disaster—when GM corn approved only for animal feed was found mixed with corn for humans. And the United States and Canada were both postponing commercial planting of GM wheat because of market jitters. A Canadian study suggested that any big wheat exporter stood to lose a third of its wheat market if it started to plant GM wheat![8]

In addition, there was still uncertainty over the supposed benefits from GM crops. Did Bt crops cut down on pesticide use? Did Roundup Ready crops reduce the overall use of herbicides? The answers depended on who did the measuring. According to an industry survey for 2001, transgenic crops have been a success. The report said herbicide-tolerant soybeans saved U.S. farmers $1 billion and a GM variety of corn raised yields by 1.58 million metric tons.[9]

> According to an industry survey for 2001, transgenic crops have been a success.

But an independent researcher, Charles Benbrook, who has followed the use of these crops for the Northwest Science and Environmental Policy Center, challenged the industry figures, arguing that they represented only tiny savings to U.S. agriculture as a whole. Benbrook said the soybean farmers didn't spend $1 billion less by using Roundup Ready. The supposed saving of $1 billion represented the estimated extra cost to GM farmers of using alternative weed killers to Monsanto's Roundup. But, he argued, farmers who don't use Roundup find other, cheaper ways of controlling weeds, including tilling their fields. According to Benbrook, Roundup users probably only break even on GM soybeans.[10] The Bt corn figures were right, but one variety's gain represented less than 1 percent of the 250 million tons of corn grown each year.

Overall, it would appear the gains have been marginal. Roundup Ready crops have reduced the average number of active chemical ingredients applied per acre but have modestly increased the average use of actual herbicide. Bt corn has had little impact on pesticide use. In any case, Benbrook says, whether GM crops reduce pesticide use is the wrong question. The real question is whether biotech can be used in a more subtle way to strengthen plants' defense mechanisms and put an end to the "pesticide treadmill" that occurs when pesticides destroy beneficial insects and, at the same time, create new, resistant pests requiring ever more pesticides.

Several studies continue to show a risk that GM crops will interbreed with wild relatives and thereby not only create GM-tainted crops but also sprout "superweeds." A team of researchers at Ohio State University showed that wild sunflowers, considered a weed by many U.S. farmers, become hardier and produce 50 percent more seeds when crossed with a GM sunflower resistant to a particular moth larva.[11] Researchers in France found gene flow between GM sugar beets and wild cousins.

Some companies have deliberately avoided such dangerous liaisons by not producing transgenic products that are promiscuous and have wild relatives growing nearby. Monsanto has not tried to improve sunflowers, which are native to the United States, for example. Even proponents of genetic engineering have warned that certain crops, such as the randy canola, might not be suitable for all fields. Planting on Canada's prairies, where sufficient space could be found to create an effective refuge between GM and non-GM crops was fine, but canola could not be trusted in more confined environments, such as Britain.

In America, an entirely new gene flow risk emerged in *biopharming*. Pharmaceutical companies realized that they could make medically important proteins more cheaply in the kernel of a corn cob than in fermentation factories. Farmers immediately saw a new and potentially profitable niche market. But grocery manufacturers took fright at the very idea. They envisioned green groups finding a gene for diarrhea in a taco shell. "Who wants a pharmaceutical in their cornflakes?" asked Rebecca Goldburg of Environmental Defense.[12] The biotech industry promised not to biopharm in major corn-producing states such as Iowa, Illinois, Indiana, and Nebraska, but grocery manufacturers wanted stricter assurances, especially after the summer of 2002, when their fears were realized.

The USDA found GM corn containing a pharmaceutical protein growing in two soybean plots in Iowa and Nebraska. The offending corn had grown from seeds left over from the test crop planted the year before by a Texas-based company, Prodigene. Exactly what genes were found and what drugs they were for remained a company secret. The USDA ordered the burning of 155 acres of surrounding corn and the quarantine of half a million bushels of harvested soybeans from the test field. The accident was potentially more disastrous than StarLink—as the food processors made clear. If the GM corn had been in a cornfield, not a soybean crop, there could have been cross-pollination. Food processors and grocers, foreseeing the possible ripple effect of such scares, were fearful of losing international markets for their popular brands.

Meanwhile the biotech companies—including Monsanto, Syngenta, Bayer, and DuPont—were doing their best to overcome the disastrous launch of biotech agriculture. Monsanto's new president and chief executive, Hendrik Verfaillie, a chemist from Belgium who rose up through the company's ranks, promised to behave "honorably, ethically, and openly" in the future, in contrast to the arrogance admitted by his predecessor, Robert Shapiro. Monsanto offered its knowledge in the rice genome for public use. But the new image did not help the company's fortunes. Monsanto's agbiotech business was badly affected by Europe's moratorium and Brazil's rejection of biotech. The company, which was still the biggest crop biotechnology firm, saw its share price cut in half during 2002. In the first nine months of 2002, the company's sales plunged more than 18 percent, to $3.45 billion from $4.25 billion. At the end of the year, Verfaillie was forced to resign.

In addition, Monsanto's leading herbicide, Roundup, was reported to be losing the battle with some weeds that had evolved a resistance to it. The company's Roundup Ready corn and canola seeds, which were resistant to the herbicide, were the cornerstone of the company's food crop business. The new weeds were not "super-weeds" in one biotech sense because they had not developed their resistance as a result of gene flow from a transgenic crop, but simply by evolution. But the lesson was clear—sameness can be a plague in agriculture whether it be mono-crops or mono-herbicides. Monsanto's rival, Syngenta, seized the opportunity to push its own products, suggesting that farmers should not limit themselves to one type of weed killer, as many had been doing with the successful Roundup.[13]

Independent biotech research continued, however. From the labs came word of several new products—from rice that maintained its yields when grown in cold, dry, or high-salt conditions that would kill normal plants, to tomatoes that acted as medicines, to potatoes that produced more protein.

The new rice was developed by a team at Cornell University.[14] The researchers experimented with a sugar named trehalose, found in a rugged desert plant known as the resurrection plant. During periods of drought the plant looks as though it has died, but after a rain shower it springs back to life. Its revival is attributed to the presence of trehalose, which is thought to protect plants in salty, arid, and cold conditions by maintaining the right balance of nutrients and minerals needed for photosynthesis. The Cornell researchers found that a pair of genes that made trehalose, borrowed from the common bacterium *E. coli*, produced the sugar in a variety of basmati rice. The growth rates of the basmati rice were just 20 percent below normal when the plants were exposed to salty, cold, or dry conditions.[15]

Meanwhile British and Dutch scientists were working on a GM tomato that produced flavonols, powerful antioxidants that fight disease by neutralizing harmful oxygen molecules that circulate in the body, damaging tissues and accelerating the aging process.[16] The researchers discovered a gene in the common petunia that produces the enzyme that makes the flavonol. The taste of the antiaging tomato was not affected, apparently.

Elsewhere there was still much apprehension about transgenic plants. Planting of GM crops was still illegal in many developing countries, not only for food safety reasons but also for international trade purposes; governments like Zambia wanted to preserve their official GM-free status.[17] When India decided to allow GM cotton to be grown in 2002, farmers saw more risk from international corporate control of seed markets than from harmful gene flow. They still believed, for example, that although Monsanto had renounced use of the Terminator technology, the company might still be able to make seeds sterile and thereby deprive Indian farmers of their traditional right to save and replant seeds from their own harvest.[18] The antibiotech lobby continued to be preoccupied by concern over this genetic trick. Although both Monsanto and Syngenta renounced the Terminator, the technology behind it was not abandoned.

And after the Terminator came the Exorcist. This was a method of killing off alien genes at the end of the plant's life cycle so that they do not appear in the pollen or the seeds and, therefore, cannot be passed to a wild relative or the next generation. The method was immediately dubbed "The Exorcist" by the masterful headline writers of the action group ETC. The technology uses a little enzyme that automatically snips off all the genes spliced into a plant at a particular stage in its development—for example, at an early stage of the development of the fruit before the pollen starts to ripen and become active.[19] The success of the method rests in the timing, of course, and some scientists are skeptical that it could ever be totally reliable. It might excise all the foreign DNA from the plant fruit but not from the seeds. The antibiotech forces saw the Exorcist more as Terminator II, a "greenwash of the issue, rather deceptive," was how the environmental group Greenwatch U.K. described it.[20] Certainly the Exorcist could be seen as just another way of preserving the seed company's intellectual property rights.

Weary from the biotech wars and with new and more detailed knowledge of plants' genomes, researchers began to take another look at traditional breeding. Tinkering with the plants' own genes, awakening slumbering genes already there rather than introducing new ones, was an attractive route that defused the "Frankenfood" argument. Because no alien genes were transferred, the new plant could not be labeled transgenic or GM.

The first plant genome to be sequenced was that of the small mustard plant, *Arabidopsis thaliana*, often used as a model for crop plants. It has prompted researchers to look at the genes that tell the plant exactly when to flower; the genes that govern plant height, root length, or the size of flowers, leaves, and seeds; and especially the genes that help the plant's natural resistance to hungry insects and creeping blight. Making plants flower earlier could extend the growing season for grains and fruits, perhaps enabling farmers to grow more than one crop a year. Even small advances in flowering time could help rice farmers. Rice needs just over six months to grow before it can be harvested, so speeding up the flowering time could allow two crops. Making plants flower later would stop vegetables such as spinach and lettuce from bolting too soon—sending up stems that sap energy.[21]

Other researchers have tried to influence a plant's growth by modifying its responses to light. When a crop plant is shaded by its neighbors, it tends to shoot upward to find the sunlight, spending energy that farmers want directed instead into making seeds. Certain proteins tell a plant when it's in the shade, and these proteins pass on the information to genes that control growth. By suppressing the activity of the shade-sensitive proteins, researchers can fool the plant into believing it is not in the shade and therefore has no reason to spend energy reaching skyward.

> "The key is how each gene regulates other genes."
> —Richard Jefferson, American microbiologist

The American microbiologist Richard Jefferson, who discovered one of the early genetic marker genes, describes the function of the genes in a genome like the keys on a piano. "Imagine the keys of a piano. There are eighty-eight keys, and I know what each key means, but it doesn't tell me how to do Beethoven, Brahms, or Mozart. Yet all of that music is locked up in those keys. The secret is in their combinations, the order, the duration, and the intensity. It's the same way with genes."[22] Jefferson gives the example of teosinte, the very different-looking wild ancestor of maize.[23] Almost all the differences between the two are caused by only a few genes, and to a huge extent the difference in shape of the two plants is associated with just one single gene. "The key is how each gene regulates other genes," says Jefferson.

Many inspiring reports have emerged. One came from Norman Borlaug, the father of the Green Revolution in Mexico and Asia. In 2002 Borlaug, at eighty-eight, was reliving his earlier days as a plant breeder cultivating new varieties of corn in ten African countries, including Ethiopia, Uganda, Mozambique, and Ghana. With the help of funds from a fellow Nobel prizewinner, former President Jimmy Carter and his Atlanta-based Carter Center, Borlaug proudly declared that he could double or triple grain production in these ten countries within three years—if public funds could be found.[24]

At Cornell one of America's leading rice breeders, Susan McCouch, has been crossing commercial rice varieties with wild species and increasing yields by 10 to 20 percent. In some cases, McCouch has found her new varieties surprisingly resistant to rice plagues even though neither of the parents had such traits.

Researchers at Sussex University in England have produced salt-tolerant tomatoes without splicing a single gene. They found that tomatoes with the ability to tolerate the most salt in their tissues were the worst at stopping salt from entering their systems, while tomatoes bad at tolerating salt had the best methods of keeping it out. So they crossbred the two kinds. The results were tomatoes that were both good at preventing salt from entering their systems and good at tolerating salt should it pass their natural barrier.

Researchers are also looking for the genes that help a plant survive when it is under stress. They have found about two thousand genes that respond to various kinds of stress—exposure to salt, for example, or drought or low temperatures. Plants that don't deal well with stress possess the genes but for some reason don't switch them on. Researchers are trying to fix the wiring, as they say.[25] They believe that within a few decades they will be able to select and reactivate genes that cultivated plants used thousands of years ago when they were growing in much rougher habitats.

The study of genomes, or *genomics*, may help scientists find defenses against the potato blight mold that caused the destruction of Ireland's potato crops in the 1840s and still ravages potato fields around the world. The disease starts with purple-black lesions on the leaves; within a week it can turn the stalk and the potato itself to mush.

The fungus-like blight has recently turned up in Russia, destroying more of the country's staple crop than at any time in memory.[26] In countries that can afford it, the blight is treated with fungicide, but the disease is adept at mutating to survive even the poisons created to obliterate it. As an alternative defense, scientists have been studying blight-resistance genes in wild potatoes. One of these genes causes cells close to the infestation to, in effect, commit suicide, so that the mold cannot spread to other parts of the plant.

In the spring of 2002 two groups of researchers reported that they had mapped the entire genome for two types of rice, giving plant breeders an exciting new tool. Although the rice genome is the smallest of the major cereals—some six times smaller than corn and thirty-seven times smaller than wheat—the agbiotech companies focused on rice because of its similarity to other cereals and because it provides a rough guide to the possible location of useful genes in all major crops.

The genome for the *indica* variety was produced by China and the University of Washington, that of the *japonica* variety by the seed conglomerate Syngenta. Not all the new and important data have become publicly available. Researchers working on the *japonica* genome have had to sign a usage agreement with the Swiss-based company, protecting the information from Syngenta's competitors. Academic researchers can use the information for research, but not for commercial use. By contrast, the *indica* sequence has been put into a publicly available genome bank for use by rich corporations and poor researchers alike.

According to these genome maps, each rice cell contains forty to sixty thousand genes, compared to thirty to forty thousand genes in each human cell. Size isn't everything. The complexity of an organism does not depend on its gene count; it's how an organism uses those genes that matters. Animals have a system of generating a variety of different protein products from a limited number of genes. Scientists liken animal genes to a Swiss Army knife, one tool with lots of applications.

At his Canberra, Australia, nonprofit institute, Richard Jefferson directs research into what he calls transgenomics—a method halfway between traditional plant breeding and genetic engineering. Jefferson is effectively trying to mimic the natural process of evolution. He believes that there is a "Jurassic Park" of diversity slumbering inside the genome. The process does involve inserting artificially created genes—from yeast or bacteria—as the triggers or promoters, but for the purpose of generating new traits from the plant's own repertoire (to use Jefferson's piano analogy), not from alien genes. Once researchers have found ways to kick-start these

> The complexity of an organism does not depend on its gene count; it's how an organism uses those genes that matters.

genes in rice, corn should not be a problem. Botanists estimate that rice and corn began evolving from a common grassy ancestor at least 60 million years ago; their genomes are still largely identical. To be provocative, Jefferson is fond of saying, "Rice is corn," a comment deemed downright inflammatory in the Corn Belt of America. The differences arise when genes are switched on or off. Instead of moving a gene from an arctic flounder to a tomato to help the tomato survive a frost, Jefferson argues, it ought to be possible to goad a rice plant into a mutation or kick-start one of its own genes to produce a desired trait.

Scientists have known for decades that corn has its own self-help genes tucked away somewhere in its genome. Known as *transposons*, a kind of jumping gene, they often increase when a plant is under stress. "One of the genome's last-ditch responses under stress is to reshuffle the deck," Cornell's McCouch observes. It's a sort of panic response to find some way of dealing with the cause of the stress—heat, drought, cold, or plague.

In theory Jefferson's work presents an alternative for developing countries that cannot afford to use genes and techniques already patented by the seed congolmerates. Jefferson calls his process a way of "inventing around" those patents. Activist green groups generally applaud him. "It's a noble effort," says Hope Shand of ETC. But the activists are still concerned that corporate control over plant genomes will eventually result in greater economic control generally over the human food chain.

Even with Jefferson's transgenomics, the wide range of parents already owned still creates roadblocks for scientists trying to work for agriculture in developing countries. The more university researchers sign exclusive deals with biotech companies—such as the five-year deal Berkeley has with Novartis—the less those researchers are free to talk to other scientists. The change has been rapid. The small band of researchers looking into the asexual trait of apomixis have held two international conferences. At the first, in 1998, almost none of them had grants that tied them to corporations and there was a reasonably free exchange of ideas. At the second, in 2001, many of the researchers had become linked to corporate deals. As one of the participants put it, "No one gave anything away. They couldn't. They were all bought."[27]

To make biotechnology work to its full potential, especially in the developing world, researchers will need to use many of the genes and techniques owned by large corporations. There are hopeful signs that companies are willing to share part of their intellectual property with poor farmers. Syngenta's deal with Potrykus and Beyer over golden rice was an early example. Monsanto's transgenic

---

To make biotechnology work to its full potential, especially in the developing world, researchers will need to use many of the genes and techniques owned by large corporations.

---

sweet potato developed by Kenyan researchers was another. But Gary Toenniessen, the director of the Rockefeller Foundation's rice biotech program, who has watched the seed companies increase their control over lab research for thirty years, puts the new corporate image into perspective. Before making these rice genome data public, Monsanto and Syngenta selected what they wanted. "They've been mining the rice resource base as fast as they could," he says. "Despite all the rhetoric, these companies are still in the business to make money."[28]

To ensure that a flow of genetic information is available to developing countries, the Rockefeller Foundation has been trying to bring corporations and leading biotech universities together to create a pool of biotech tools—genes as well as laboratory techniques—that could be used free of royalties by researchers engaged in work specifically for poor countries. Others would like to see a radical restructuring of the patent system itself, perhaps one that would provide only limited protection for plant varieties, leaving genes and lab techniques free to be used for further research.

Until now I have deliberately avoided Malthusian discussions about biotech agriculture. Such debates mostly play straight into the hands of partisans. One side suggests that biotech is a magic bullet that will "feed the world"—in the memorable words of the

Nobel prizewinning agronomist Norman Borlaug. The other side says that there is no such thing as a magic bullet for such a complex problem. There is already enough food in the world to keep people from starving. The solution, this side says, is not to produce more food but to enable people to afford what's available. The argument usually ends right there. It would be wrong, however, to leave a book about the future of food without taking the next step.[29]

In his 1798 *Essay on the Principle of Population*, the English clergyman Thomas Malthus foresaw an overcrowded future, a world with more people than food, resulting in global starvation and limits to the world's population. In those days, the earth's population was about 800 million. Today the population has grown to 6 billion, proving Malthus wrong, at least about upper limit to the number of human beings on the planet. During the nineteenth and twentieth centuries, with the help of new technologies, the amount of acreage cultivated across the globe became equal to the size of South America. We have doused those cleared fields with millions of tons of toxic chemicals in order to boost crop yields to meet the demand for food. While Malthus was wrong about the numbers, he was right about some people always being hungry. At the beginning of the twenty-first century, 800 million people still go to bed hungry every night.

By 2050 or so, the world population could start to level off at about 9 billion. Most of the increase in population will be in the developing world, where so many depend on rice as the basis of their diet. Yet rice yields have been stagnant for the last fifteen years in rice-producing countries such as Japan, Korea, and China. Increased yields have depended in the past on additional fertilizers, but in the fantastic yield increases of the Green Revolution, fertilizer is approaching its limit. Unused arable land is scarce, water supplies are dangerously low, and soils are impoverished. All the signs point to a future in which the world's poor will not be able to afford enough food to live on and in which the distribution system in undeveloped countries will not improve sufficiently to distribute food that is available.[30]

The question is, to what extent can biotechnology help in making up the shortfall? More than a decade ago, when young scientists were attracted to biotech agriculture, it promised two things: a reduction in the amount of pesticide use and the creation of an agriculture that would enable farmers, poor farmers especially, to produce food in a sustainable and more rational way. The new technology still holds out a possibility of cutting back on harmful chemicals, but the second promise has not turned out the way many had hoped. As one scientist from the early biotech era observes, "It got turned around on us. The technology became aligned with the corporate sector, with its objectives and its vision of the future. A lot of us who realized that it could service the different vision of sustainable agriculture are still struggling to give life to that alternative view."

Big corporations hijacked the technology, buying company after company primarily to expand their portfolios of biotech patents. Instead of inspiring inventors, as patents were originally intended to do, this intellectual property grab tended to exclude all but the rich corporate laboratories. Scientists had far less time, or inclination, to care about the public good, and those who saw biotech as a way to feed the world were hard to find. Vandana Shiva observed that the technology itself was seen as being "above society."[31]

There is no point in producing food that people refuse to eat. Nobody has learned this bitter lesson more thoroughly than biotech corporations and American farmers. The only way biotechnology can be switched back on track is by getting the public more involved. This means restoring the confidence of the grocery shopper by labeling GM foods. It means giving the public an opportunity to listen to reasoned arguments, no matter how complex the issue. With cloning and X-factoring and matrixing all part of public lore, most ordinary people already have some grasp of genes and genomes. So far, the public debate has been beneath them. Part of the blame rests with the companies who tried to sneak their products onto the market without telling people about them. Another part rests with those activist groups who took raising awareness beyond its usefulness and turned it into scare-mongering.

Biotech agriculture is another step in the evolution of human food, a process of change that began slowly and now, in evolutionary terms, moves at mach speed. The changes are not inherently unsafe, nor are the companies that produce them inherently evil. Transgenic foods have been eaten by contented and discerning consumers in America for a decade. Moreover, the promise of producing more food in African deserts or the wetlands of Asia is worth the time and money spent on these new seeds.

There are plenty of things for the public to worry about, however. One concern is how government agencies study and approve new seeds. In addition, old seeds must be preserved in public seed banks. Companies need to be more generous with patents that can be used to produce food in countries where people are starving. Genetic engineering has a pragmatic and realistic use for developing countries but only if it is properly integrated into the different agricultural systems. Finally, the strategic planners of world agriculture must bring an end to a system that through farm subsidies has long been rigged in favor of rich countries. Without this reform, poor nations have no hope of being able to compete in world grain markets.

The tinkering with genes in our food is not going to stop because some people consider the science a little freaky or believe that it has gone too far. Mendel's peas were revolutionary in their way in 1865. So were the modified tomatoes of 1992 and the golden rice of 2000, which may still help to prevent blindness in poor regions of the world. These GM groceries are not Frankenfoods any more than a person with a transplanted heart is today's Frankenstein. They are scientific creations full of both promise and potential hazard. These experimental foods deserve respect from those who discover them, call for more caution from those who regulate them and grow them, and finally, at the end of this real food chain, demand close study by those of us who eat them.

Notes

1. Richard Ragan, WFP representative quoted by PanAfrica News Agency, August 13, 2002.

2. The Biosafety Protocol comes into force when fifty nations have ratified it. At the time of writing, thirty-seven had done so, including the fifteen nations of the EU, several African nations, and India, New Zealand, Austria, and Denmark.

3. Devlin Kuyek, "Genetically Modified Crops in African Culture," GRAIN, August 2002. Reference from R. Paarlberg, "Policies Towards GM Crops in Kenya," in *Governing the GM Crop Revolution: Policy Choices for Developing Countries.* 2020 Vision Food, Agriculture and the Environment; discussion paper 33, December 2000. See also Kristin Dawkins, "Biotech from Seattle to Montreal and Beyond: The Battle Royale of the 21st Century," a paper from The Institute for Agriculture and Trade Policy, Minneapolis, February 2000.

4. Ann Veneman, USDA statement, August 30, 2002.

5. Hope Shand, Pew Initiative on Food and Biotechnology, Spotlight, Of Famine and Food Aid: GM Food Internationally, October 2002.

6. "Poverty and Transgenic Crops," *Nature*, August 8, 2002, 569.

7. Simon Robinson, "To Eat or Not to Eat: As Zambia Starves and the E.U. Battle over Genetically Modified Food Aid in Africa," *Time* (European edition), December 2, 2002.

8. Ibid., 7.

9. Kurt Kleiner, "Fields of Gold: Biotech Cash Benefits May Not Be What They Seem," *New Scientist,* June 22, 2002: 11. Leonard Gianessi, National Center for Food and Agricultural Policy, partly funded by Monsanto and the Biotechnology Industry Organization.

10. Ibid. Also Charles Benbrook, The Bt Premium Price: What Does It Buy? The Impact of Extra By Corn Seed Costs on Farmer Earnings and Corporate Finances, Paper, Benbrook Consulting Services, Sandpoint, Idaho, February 2002.

11. Andy Coghlan, "Weeds Do Well out of Modified Crops," *New Scientist*, August 17, 2002:11.

12. Rebecca Goldburg, quoted by Bob Holmes, "Dangerous Liaisons," *New Scientist,* August 31, 2002. 38–41.

13. Andrew Pollack, "Widely Used Crop Herbicide Is Losing Weed Resistance," *New York Times*, January 14, 2003: Cl.

14. Proceedings of the National Academy of Sciences, www.PNAS online, DOI:10.1073/pnas.252637799; and BBC News online. http://news.bbc.co.uk/2/hi/science/nature/1251295.stm.

15. Andy Coghlan, "Sweet Genes Help Rice in a Drought," *New Scientist*, November 30, 2002, 10.

16. BBC News Online, "GM Tomato to Fight Disease," May 2, 2001. Research led by Martin Verhoyen, Unilever Research, Sharnbrook, U.K. http://www.biotech-info.net/GM_tomato.html.

17. Joel Cohen and Robert Paarlberg, "Explaining Restricted Approval and Availability of GM Crops in Developing Countries," *AgBiotechNet*, October 2002, 6.

18. Ibid., 6. Monsanto had renounced use of the technology after intervention by Gordon Conway, president of the Rockefeller Foundation, but the fear persisted.

19. Philip Cohen, "Begone Evil Genes," *New Scientist*, July 6, 2002, 33–36. The Exorcist was the brainchild of Pim Stemmer and his colleague Robert Keenan, of the biotech company Maxygen of Redwood City, California.

20. Sue Mayer of Greenwatch U.K. in Philip Cohen, "Begone Evil Genes," *New Scientist*, July 6, 2002: 33.

21. Anne Simon Moffat, Can Genetically Modified Crops Grow Greener?" *Science*, October 13, 2000, 253.

22. Author interviews, April 2001; June 2001. See also Ehsan Masood, Opinion interview, *New Scientist*, October 21, 2000; Elizabeth Finkel, "Australian Center Develops Tools for Developing World," *Science*, September 1999; Barnaby J. Feder, "New Method of Altering Plants Is Aimed at Sidestepping Critics," *New York Times*, Science Times, February 29, 2000, 1.

23. John Doebly, *Nature*, March 18, 1999, 236.

24. Scot Kilman and Roger Thurow, "Africa Could Grow Enough Food Itself: Should It?" *Wall Street Journal*, December 3, 2002, 1 and 14.

25. Andy Goghlan et al., "Beyond Organics," *New Scientist*, May 18, 2002, 33–47.

26. Glenn Garelick, "Taking the Bite out of Potato Blight," *Science*, November 29, 2002; 1702–4.

27. Yves Savidan, author interview, April 25, 2001. See also Charles Benbrook, "Who Controls and Who Will Benefit from Plant Genomics" paper to AAAS annual meeting, Washington, D.C., February 19, 2000.

28. Justin Gillis, "Cultivating a New Image, Firms Give Away Data, Patent Rights on Crops," *Washington Post*, May 23, 2002.

29. Jeffrey Burkhardt, "Biotechnology's Future Benefits: Prediction or Promise?" *AgBioForum* 5(2): 20–24; Peter Raven, "Presidential Address, AAAS," *Science*, August 9, 2002; Susan McCouch, author interview, October 29, 2002; Rebecca Goldburg, author interview, 2002; Calestous Juma, "How Not to Save the World," *New Scientist*, September 28, 2002, 24; Anthony Trewavas, "Malthus Foiled and Foiled Again," *Nature*, August 8, 2002, 668–70; David Tilman et al., "Agricultural Sustainability and Intensive Production Practices," *Nature*, August 8, 2002, 671–77; R. Hails, "Assessing the Risks Associated with New Agricultural Practices," *Nature*, August 8, 2002, 685–88.

30. Klaus Leisinger, Karin Schmidt, and Rajul Pandya-Lorch, "Six Billion and Counting. Population and Food Security in the 21st Century" International Food Policy Research Institute, 2002, 8–9, and Per Pinstrup-Anderson and Ebbe Schiøler, *Seed of Contention*, 68–71.

31. Vandana Shiva, "The Seed and the Spinning Wheel: The UNDP as Biotech Salesman," Reflections on the Human Development Reprint, July 25, 2001.

Debate Grows Over Biotech Food

By Justin Gillis
The Washington Post, November 30, 2003

When the people by the lake began to starve, they fell back on the knowledge of their ancestors. They picked poisonous fruits from the bush and boiled them for three days to eliminate the toxin, concocting a barely palatable dish. But sometimes hungry children would sneak a taste early, villagers said, and the poison would make them ill.

Kebby Kamota, father of 11, could take it no longer. "Three days! Three days!" he shouted, explaining how long his children would sometimes go without food as a drought worsened last year. "When I saw my children getting hungry, it was not easy for me."

Even as the bellies of the children ached, bags of relief corn sat in a warehouse, sealed tight, in this village [Munyama, Zambia] on the shores of Lake Kariba. The U.S. government said the corn, a variety created by modern biotechnology and grown in the United States, was safe to eat. The Zambian government wasn't so sure, and it ordered the food locked up even after aid groups had shipped it to stricken villages.

So Kamota rounded up a mob that forced its way into the warehouse and distributed corn to scores of village families. A feast ensued. With that momentary act of defiance, the villagers of Munyama not only restocked their barren larders, they unwittingly became symbols in the long-running fight between Europe and the United States over agricultural biotechnology.

To biotechnology advocates, the villagers, along with people who broke into other Zambian warehouses last year, showed the human costs of an irrational new technophobia, centered in Europe and intent on blocking the development of gene-altered crops.

To skeptics of biotechnology, the Zambian villagers became a symbol of the American government's willingness to use destitute Africans as pawns in pressing the interests of Western corporations.

The debate over this technology has become a leading issue in international relations, subject of a huge trade battle. Wall Street is watching anxiously as it presses companies to recoup their massive biotech investments by selling more seeds. Environmental advocates are marching in the streets to oppose the crops. Even the Vatican is weighing the issue, recently opening a debate about which is the moral course.

The fight has turned into an intense, emotional struggle over the very nature of food and the future of agriculture. And it is a fight now playing out in the capitals and remotest villages of Africa, the continent with the most difficulty in supplying food for all citizens.

As European resistance stiffened in recent years, the biotech industry began to argue that genetically altered crops offer a prime hope for helping Africa solve its agricultural problems and feed itself.

The biotech-for-Africa argument reached a crescendo over the summer in Washington, at the convention of the Biotechnology Industry Organization, when President Bush and various members of his administration gave speeches endorsing the industry line.

"For the sake of a continent threatened by famine, I urge the European governments to end their opposition to biotechnology," Bush told the trade group. "We should encourage the spread of safe, effective biotechnology to win the fight against global hunger."

European political leaders reacted angrily to the suggestion that they were willing to starve Africans, and they have accused American companies of deliberately exaggerating the potential role of the technology in solving Africa's problems. People with long experience in African agriculture said that only a subset of the continent's food problems are solvable, even in principle, by genetic engineering.

"They tried to lie to people, trying to force it upon people," the European environment commissioner, Margot Wallstrom, said recently. She and other European leaders have argued that, for all the rhetoric about helping Africa, relatively little biotech money has gone into researching the staple crops, such as cassava and bananas, on which millions of Africans depend.

"When they argued about feeding the starving, why did they not start out with these products?" she said. "Feeding the starving shareholders, yes, but not others."

Many citizens in Europe, battered by a series of food-safety scandals, perceive no clear benefits to themselves from the technology and are worried that the crops might be harmful.

Some governments have been persuaded in principle by such arguments. But others have resisted biotech crops for fear adopting them would hurt their ability to sell exports to Europe. Only five countries—the United States, Argentina, China, Canada and South Africa—have aggressively adopted the crops.

Earlier this year, the United States filed suit in the World Trade Organization to overturn a de facto European moratorium on new crop approvals. There's talk the Europeans may lift the suspension before the end of the year, but even so, it's not clear European consumers will buy biotech food.

For both sides of the debate, Africa has become a kind of proving ground, a stage on which they hope to claim the moral high ground. The reason is plain enough: Of the 800 million undernourished people on the Earth, a quarter live in the part of Africa that lies below the Sahara Desert, the world's greatest concentration of food insecurity.

Largely lost in this transatlantic shouting match have been the voices of Africans themselves. Do they want the technology, and is it really going to solve many of the problems that haunt their continent?

Trickling Down

If biotechnology is ever going to transform agriculture in Africa, you wouldn't know it from the evidence on the ground today. A recent journey through four African countries, and telephone interviews with people in several more, turned up evidence of success only in South Africa. There, both commercial farmers and poor, subsistence farmers are growing biotech crops, and they appear to be reaping economic gains.

But even in South Africa, the crops that have been successful were developed in America, and have essentially trickled down to African farmers. Projects are underway across Africa to use genetic engineering to improve staple crops on which tens of millions of poor people depend, such as cassava, cowpeas and sweet potatoes. But after more than a decade of work, not a single program has led to government approval and release of a new variety.

Ugandan banana biologist W.K. Tushemereirwe hopes to change that. "I am in the group that thinks biotechnology has a role to play in Africa's future, particularly if it focuses on developing our indigenous crops, not replacing them with new crops," he said in an interview.

Outside the Ugandan capital of Kampala, white-coated scientists working in his unit hunkered down recently at a laboratory bench in a new government laboratory devoted to genetic engineering. In this mountainous African country that straddles the equator, as much as any place in Africa, the advocates of modern biotechnology aim to prove their claims about helping the poor.

Bananas are the world's fourth most-important crop, after rice, corn and wheat, based on the number of people who depend on them as a staple. Starchy bananas, similar to plantains, are a vital food in Uganda and throughout the tropics. But, as a result in part of growing trade links that help spread plant diseases, bananas are under attack from a host of pests, and conventional efforts to combat them have been only partially successful.

With support from President Yoweri Museveni, the Ugandan government recently opened one of the most advanced biotech research laboratories in Africa to work on bettering the banana. Yet the work has only just begun—making the banana crisis one of several instances where the biotech industry's public-relations campaign has outrun scientific achievement.

Industry meetings have repeatedly highlighted the development, in Belgium, of a banana variety resistant to one serious disease, black sigatoka. But that plant is a lowland variety that would not be suitable for growing in mountainous Uganda. Belgian and Ugandan researchers have struck up a collaboration, but even if the research goes smoothly, they said, they could easily be a decade away from having an improved highland banana.

Western agricultural companies have pledged to support other projects scattered around Africa. Monsanto Co. has backed efforts in Kenya toward a virus-resistant sweet potato, but after a decade of work, field tests were disappointing. Biotech advocates said government approval of any improved African crop remains at least three to five years away.

Some of the problems are political. Amid global controversy, many African countries have been slow to put in place the necessary regulations and test capability for biotech crops. All sides agree that new crops are going to have to go through arduous reviews, since the environmental risks they entail vary from place to place.

"Yes, this technology has concerns—it has some risks," said Luke E. Mumba, dean of natural sciences at the University of Zambia and an advocate of biotechnology. "We must look at each product on a case-by-case basis. There should not be a wholesale rejection of say 'no' to biotechnology."

Many of the publicly funded, pro-biotech agricultural researchers doing the work said that money, not politics, has been their biggest problem. Companies have begun to contribute valuable patents and technical help for African projects, they said, but the industry's assistance has not been accompanied by any large infusion of cash.

The Belgian work has gotten "very, very, very little" support from industry, said the lead researcher, Rony Swennen, of the Catholic University of Leuven. Governments are starting to help, but still, money is so tight he can afford to train only one Ugandan researcher at a time in the most critical gene-engineering techniques.

"From different sources everywhere, I have to scratch a little bit of money," Swennen said. "I believe that genetic engineering can contribute a lot, but it's lying on the shelf. It's really a shame."

Some scientists said African farming faces more pressing needs. Hans R. Herren, director general of the International Centre of Insect Physiology and Ecology, in Nairobi, has worked in Africa for 25 years, and he won the World Food Prize for a program to control the cassava mealybug, a threat to the staple crop of 200 million Africans. Asked, as a mental exercise, to design a battle plan for solving Africa's agricultural problems, he said that biotechnology would certainly be on it—but well down the list.

"I think it is wrong to sort of say that we need genetically modified crops to feed Africa," he said. "We need many other things first. You would need better agronomy, you need better fertilizer, you need better crop management. You have to make sure there are markets, there's storage, there are roads, there are trucks. Maybe in 15 or 20 years when we have solved all these other things, biotechnology will have something to contribute."

Yielding Profits

It is summertime in the southern hemisphere, and a fierce, hot wind blew across a district of South Africa called the Makhathini Flats in the KwaZulu-Natal province. This poor, rural area is one of the few places in Africa where farmers are already growing gene-altered crops. Far down a dirt road, a man named T.J. Buthelezi recently sat in a sandy yard with his back to the wind and told the story of his rising fortunes.

KwaZulu-Natal is home to the Zulus, the proud tribe that once humbled the British empire in battle. Today, more pride than money is in evidence there. Farms are tiny, people tend to plow with donkeys or oxen and spray their crops with tanks strapped to their backs, and they harvest by hand. Electricity, cars and indoor plumbing are rare. Buthelezi lived in a thatched-roof mud hut not long ago. Behind him as he spoke stood a new house made of concrete blocks, with a metal roof.

Buthelezi said he was wary, a few years back, when a man from the local cotton company began pushing a new type of biotech seed, developed in America, that was twice as expensive as local cotton. But he was curious, so he planted some of the seed near his regular cotton. He was stunned by the differences.

Cotton is an arduous crop to grow, with African farmers typically spraying expensive, dangerous chemicals 10 or more times a season to fight off fast-moving worms and other pests. That is a huge constraint on Zulu farmers—lacking modern equipment, they can grow only as much cotton as one or two people can spray by hand in a day, limiting their farms to a few acres.

The new crop, Buthelezi said, required far less spraying, only a couple of times the whole season in his case. The yields were higher, and despite seed costs, the overall economics were much more favorable than with regular cotton. He realized that he could plant bigger crops, eventually giving him the money to build a new home and send his children to school.

"This is the field that feeds my family," Buthelezi said on a tour of the plot where he ran that first experiment. "This is the field that took my kids into school. This is the field that built my houses. I was able to sit down with my wives"—he has five of them—"and say, 'What are we going to do with this money?'"

Buthelezi heads a farmer association and has spoken in Washington in favor of the biotech cotton, drawing accusations from environmental groups that he has become an industry shill. But researchers at Britain's University of Reading, in the most elaborate study of its kind yet done in Africa, have verified the economic benefits of biotech cotton. And a half-dozen farmers interviewed in the Makhathini Flats told tales similar to Buthelezi's. The Reading researchers found evidence that the new crop is safer, too—hospital admissions for pesticide poisoning, an occupational hazard for cotton farmers, are falling.

Cotton is not a food crop, of course, but the extra cash the biotech cotton is throwing off has allowed farmers to buy the food they need. "Before, my wife used to tell me that we've got to plant a field of vegetables there and there, because we didn't have money to buy food," Buthelezi said. "Now, we do."

And the whole cycle may be starting over, this time with corn, in another part of KwaZulu-Natal near the town of Hlabisa. Farmers there have just started planting biotech corn and said they, too, are seeing benefits. Poor farmers here and in the Makhathini Flats tend to buy their seeds each year on the commercial market. Biotech seeds can cost twice as much as traditional ones but the crops they produce require less fertilizer and pesticides, and less work to maintain—generating higher margins.

Richard Sithole, a corn and potato farmer, showed off the new house he said he was able to build with improved profits from his corn crop.

"The biotech maize seed is very expensive, but looking at the costs for labor and chemicals, I think it is less expensive overall," he said, speaking through a translator in IsiZulu.

Many of the cotton farmers in the Flats are women, and they said the easier-to-grow cotton has been particularly helpful for them, since the spray tanks they strap to their backs are smaller than those for men. Doris Gumbi vibrated with energy as she showed off her farm. She is the sole support for her husband—he is old and ill, she explained—and four children. With the new cotton, she said, a woman farming alone is able to make a living for her family.

Behind her stood a new house, with a metal roof, that she said she built with the profits from biotech cotton. She laughed about her leaky old hut, standing nearby. A telephone wire and an electric cable dropped down from a pole to the house—the Gumbi family has joined the modern age.

She dipped her head shyly as she described her hopes for the future, unveiling a plan that would have been out of reach for a small Zulu farmer just a few years ago. "I want to buy a tractor," she said.

Nearing Starvation

In a place called Munyama, situated on steep hillsides by the shores of Lake Kariba, in southern Zambia, villagers live in mud huts and modest concrete houses, scratching out a living from the soil. No telephones ring. No electric lights pierce the darkness. Roads are all but impassable, and to reach the village, one travels by boat, dodging hippopotamuses at the water's edge. It would be hard to find a place farther removed from the modern world, yet here, last year, the debate over new technology reached a kind of flash point.

Crops failed in much of southern Africa because of drought, and southern Zambia, drier and hotter than the rest of the country, was particularly hard-hit. The Zambian government asked the World Food Program, a United Nations agency, for help. Calling on donor governments, including the United States, the food agency began bringing in corn, a staple food for many people in Zambia. Like a third of the corn grown in the United States, the relief corn was genetically engineered to resist worms.

Richard F. Ragan, director of the World Food Program in Zambia, said he asked government leaders in advance if they had any problem with such biotech food, and was told no. The Zambian vice president at the time, Enoch P. Kavindele, declared that if the food was good enough for Americans, it was good enough for Zambians. But after the food was on its way to villages, the Zambian political opposition questioned its safety, and a controversy erupted.

Over weeks of discussion, many leaders in Zambia came to fear the country could damage its long-term economic prospects for short-term relief. They worried that villagers would plant some of

---

Crops failed in much of southern Africa because of drought, and southern Zambia, drier and hotter than the rest of the country, was particularly hard-hit.

---

the corn, potentially transferring altered genetic material to local crops of baby corn, a product that Zambians grow for export. One of the few development strategies open to African countries is to market such high-value farm products to Europe, which is accessible from Africa by air freight. The Zambian leaders also focused on theoretical worries about the safety of eating biotech crops.

The government grew so concerned it ordered the corn sequestered, essentially freezing the food-aid pipeline for three months. Even corn already distributed to villages was ordered held under lock and key. And eventually, despite international appeals, the Zambian government decided it would not allow such corn into the country.

Recently, a group of Munyama villagers sat in a circle under a neem tree, recounting last year's crisis. Roosters crowed, goats bleated, and the lake lapped gently at the shoreline a few feet away as they spoke through a translator in Tonga, their native language.

The villagers said they planted vegetables and corn early in the season, but these wilted in the drought, and they could not catch enough fish from the lake to feed everyone. As the situation worsened, they said, some people collapsed of hunger, though none died. They resorted to eating poisonous fruits, known as "sozwe," that must be stewed for days to render them palatable.

When they heard that American corn had come to the village through an aid group, Harvest Help, they grew hopeful. But then their hearts sank when they learned the government had sequestered it. They had eaten American corn meal—they call it mealie meal—of that type before with no problem.

"As we were nearing starvation, there was actually food in the storeroom, and we knew where that food was," recalled Kebby Kamota, the farmer with 11 children. "So a small group of us decided we should come and demand the key by force."

They accosted an aid worker, Bernard Munyey. "They said, 'If you want to remain in peace, not in pieces, you will give us the key,'" said Munyey, who eventually relented. Recounting the feast that ensued, the Munyama villagers smiled and laughed.

The police came, but merely issued warnings. And Kamota, though regretful about resorting to force, said he would do it again.

"I'm actually glad I took that decision," he said. "If I had not done that, some people were going to die."

An Array of Barriers

Whatever the sentiment in the remote villages of Zambia, back in the capital, Lusaka, the country's leaders remain among the most skeptical in Africa toward biotech crops.

In an interview at his office, the agriculture minister, Mundia Sikatana, said that even putting aside concerns about food safety and the environment, biotech crops would do little to solve the structural problems of Zambian agriculture.

Zambia has vast tracts of arable land, sunshine and 40 percent of the water reserves in sub-Saharan Africa. But it also has a recent history as a socialist, centralized economy, one kept alive for many years by revenue from a copper industry now in the doldrums. Economic liberalization has not brought much prosperity.

Sikatana outlined a daunting array of agricultural barriers, many typical of the problems throughout sub-Saharan Africa. Few of them sounded amenable to solution by geneticists.

The country lacks sufficient facilities to store crops or adequate roads to transport them. The farm-credit system is inadequate, Sikatana said, and farmers don't consistently get critical supplies, such as fertilizer.

As last year's crisis worsened, Sikatana—newly sworn into office—pledged that if the country did not produce a bumper crop this year, he would resign. It did, thanks in part to crash programs to help farmers, and he didn't. Sikatana is pushing a whole series of plans, from winter crops to irrigation to fertilizer distribution, to improve the country's output. But the most important task, he said, is to erase the old socialist mentality.

"People would be given coupons to go and line up for free food, so why would they grow anything?" he said. "It wasn't easy when I called the Zambians lazy. I came under attack. But the mind-set started changing."

Indeed, people across Zambia appear determined to turn the country's agriculture around and show the world they can feed themselves—without biotech crops. A can-do spirit has taken hold even in places like Munyama, where villagers are experimenting with irrigation and winter crops.

Environmental groups have argued that donors like the United States could easily supply non-biotech food relief to countries wary of gene-altered crops. But there's strong political resistance in the United States to letting anti-biotech forces score a symbolic victory.

American biotech advocates have asked why Zambia would let people starve to serve a tendentious objection to modern technology. But in interviews, several Zambian leaders turned that question around, asking whether in another crisis the United States would be willing to let Zambians starve to make a point

"We have had to tell people, 'The outside world has no responsibility for our failures,'" Sikatana said. "'They will not feed us—we must feed ourselves with what we grow.'"

Genetic Engineering Is
Not the Answer

By Sean McDonagh
America, May 2, 2005

In 1992 the then-chief executive of Monsanto, Robert Shapiro, told the Harvard Business Review that genetically modified crops will be necessary to feed a growing world population. He predicted that if population levels were to rise to 10 billion, humanity would face two options: either open up new land for cultivation or increase crop yields. Since the first choice was not feasible, because we were already cultivating marginal land and in the process creating unprecedented levels of soil erosion, we would have to choose genetic engineering. This option, Shapiro argued, was merely a further improvement on the agricultural technologies that gave rise to the Green Revolution that saved Asia from food shortages in the 1960's and 1970's.

Genetically engineered crops might seem an ideal solution. Yet both current data and past examples show problems and provoke doubts as to their necessity.

The Green Revolution

The Green Revolution involved the production of hybrid seeds by crossing two genetically distant parents, which produced an offspring plant that gave increased yield. Critics of genetic engineering question the accepted wisdom that its impact has been entirely positive. Hybrid seeds are expensive and heavily reliant on fertilizers and pesticides. And because they lose their vigor after the first planting, the farmer must purchase new seeds for each successive planting.

In his book *Geopolitics and the Green Revolution*, John H. Perkins describes the environmentally destructive and socially unjust aspects of the Green Revolution. One of its most important negative effects, he says, is that it has contributed to the loss of three-quarters of the genetic diversity of major food crops and that the rate of erosion continues at close to 2 percent per year. The fundamental importance of genetic diversity is illustrated by the fact that when a virulent fungus began to destroy wheat fields in the United States and Canada in 1950, plant breeders staved off disaster by cross-breeding five Mexican wheat varieties with 12 imported ones. In the process they created a new strain that was able to resist so-called "stem rust." The loss of these varieties would have been a catastrophe for wheat production globally.

The Terminator Gene

The development by a Monsanto-owned company of what is benignly called a Technology Protection System—a more apt name is terminator technology—is another reason for asserting that the feed-the-world argument is completely spurious. Genetically engineered seeds that contain the terminator gene self-destruct after the first crop. Once again, this forces farmers to return to the seed companies at the beginning of each planting season. If this technology becomes widely used, it will harm the two billion subsistence farmers who live mainly in the poor countries of the world. Sharing seeds among farmers has been at the very heart of subsistence farming since the domestication of staple food crops 11,000 years ago. The terminator technology will lock farmers into a regime of buying genetically engineered seeds that are herbicide tolerant and insect resistant, tethering them to the chemical treadmill.

On an ethical level, a technology that, according to Professor Richard Lewontin of Harvard University, "introduces a 'killer' transgene that prevents the germ of the harvested grain from developing" must be considered grossly immoral. It is a sin against the poor, against previous generations who freely shared their knowledge of plant life with us, against nature itself and finally against the God of all creativity. To set out deliberately to create seeds that self-destruct is an abomination no civilized society should tolerate. Furthermore, there is danger that the terminator genes could spread to neighboring crops and to the wild and weedy relatives of the plant that has been engineered to commit suicide. This would jeopardize the food security of many poor people.

The current situation promoting genetically modified organisms also means supporting the patenting of living organisms—both crops and animals. I find it difficult to understand the support that Cardinal Renato Martino, prefect of the Pontifical Council for Justice and Peace, seems to be giving to genetically modified organisms, given the Catholic Church's strong pro-life position. In my book *Patenting Life? Stop!* I argue that "patenting life is a fundamental attack on the understanding of life as interconnected, mutually dependent and a gift of God to be shared with everyone. Patenting opts for an atomized, isolated understanding of life." The Indian scientist and activist Dr. Vandana Shiva believes that patented crops will lead to food dictatorship by a handful of northern transnational corporations. This would certainly be a recipe for hunger and starvation—in conflict with Catholic social teaching on food and agriculture.

No Higher Yield, No Reduction in Chemicals

Early in 2003 a researcher at the Institute of Development Studies at Sussex University in England published an analysis of the G.M.O. crops that biotech companies are developing for Africa. Among the plants studied were cotton, maize and the sweet potato. The G.M.O. research on the sweet potato is now approaching its 12th year and has involved the work of 19 scientists; to date it has cost $6 million. Results indicated that yield has increased by 18 percent. On the other hand, conventional sweet potato breeding, working with a small budget, has produced a virus-resistant variety with a 100 percent yield increase.

Claims that G.M.O.'s lead to fewer chemicals in agriculture are also being challenged. A comprehensive study using U.S. government data on the use of chemicals on genetically engineered crops was carried out by Charles Benbrook, head of the Northwest Science and Environmental Policy Center in Sandpoint, Idaho. He found

---

People are hungry because they do not have access to food production processes or the money to buy food.

---

that when G.M.O.'s were first introduced, they needed 25 percent fewer chemicals for the first three years. But in 2001, 5 percent more chemicals were sprayed compared with conventional crop varieties. Dr. Benbrook stated: "The proponents of biotechnology claim G.M.O. varieties substantially reduce pesticide use. While true in the first few years of widespread planting, it is not the case now. There's now clear evidence that the average pound of herbicide applied per acre planted to herbicide-tolerant varieties have increased compared to the first few years."

Toward a Solution

Hunger and famine around the world have more to do with the absence of land reform, social inequality, bias against women farmers and the scarcity of cheap credit and basic agricultural tools than with lack of agribusiness super-seeds. This fact was recognized by those who attended the World Food Summit in Rome in November 1996. People are hungry because they do not have access to food production processes or the money to buy food. Brazil, for example, is the third largest exporter of food in the world, yet one-fifth of its population, over 30 million people, do not have enough food to eat. Clearly hunger there is not due to lack of food but to the unequal distribution of wealth and the fact that a huge number of people are landless.

Do the proponents of genetically engineered food think that agribusiness companies will distribute such food free to the hungry poor who have no money? There was food in Ireland during the famine in the 1840's, for example, but those who were starving had no access to it or money to buy it.

As a Columban missionary in the Philippines, I saw something similar during the drought caused by El Niño in 1983. There was a severe food shortage among the tribal people in the highlands of Mindanao. The drought destroyed their cereal crops, and they could no longer harvest food in the tropical forest because it had been cleared during the previous decades. Even during the height of the drought, an agribusiness corporation was exporting tropical fruit from the lowlands. There was also sufficient rice and corn in the lowlands, but the tribal people did not have the money to buy it. Had it not been for food aid from nongovernmental organizations, many of the tribal people would have starved.

In 1990 the World Food Program at Brown University calculated that if the global food harvest over the previous few years were distributed equitably among all the people of the world, it could provide a vegetarian diet for over 6 billion people. In contrast, a meat-rich diet, favored by affluent countries and currently available to the global elite, could feed only 2.6 billion people. Human society is going to be faced with the option of getting protein from plants or from animals. If we opt for animal protein, the consequence will be a much less equitable world, with increasing levels of human misery.

Those who wish to banish hunger should address the social and economic inequalities that create poverty and not claim that a magic-bullet technology will solve all the problems.

Feed Starving Masses,
Not Irrational Fears

USA TODAY, MAY 25, 2004

Some 842 million people—13% of the world's population—don't have enough food to eat each day. Millions of them face starvation in Africa because of droughts and armed conflicts in countries that include Sudan, Angola and Uganda.

In one sense, that's an old story—so old, it makes even sympathetic eyes glaze over. But it could have a new happy ending that, remarkably, has yet to be written. While the script promises a reliable, cheap food supply for all who are hungry, some fear that outcome the way villagers were terrified by Mary Shelley's Frankenstein monster.

In fact, fearful environmentalists and their political allies call the solution "Frankenfood," crops genetically altered to resist disease, pests and drought, or staples engineered to add nutrients. Such crops could transform health in the poorest nations, the United Nations' Food and Agricultural Organization said in a report last week. Biotech rice alone could prevent 500,000 cases of blindness and 2 million children's deaths each year as a result of vitamin A deficiency.

Yet most of Europe, where a purist view of agriculture reigns, has banned biofoods because of health and environmental worries. That has caused some African nations to reject U.N. donations of foods containing bioengineered seeds; they fear their agricultural exports would be shut out of Europe.

The U.N. report challenged European myths about genetic modification, which has existed since our ancestors used microorganisms to make bread, wine and cheese. No serious illnesses tied to these foods have been documented, it notes. In the U.S., most foods are genetically modified in some way and must meet rigid safety standards.

Technology is never risk-free, but given the minimal risks, denying the food to starving people defies reason and conscience.

Major biotech firms, under political pressure to do more to tackle world hunger, are addressing the problem. They have shared proprietary data with researchers across the world and field-tested many crops in poor countries, where the companies' profit potential is limited.

The biggest hurdle is the lack of acceptance because of opponents' scare tactics or unfounded fears:

In the midst of a famine that killed millions, Zambia and Zimbabwe in 2002 turned away corn donated by the U.N. because some contained bioengineered seeds. Zambia, whose president called the crops "poison," still bans biotech foods. Sudan, Mozambique, Angola and Zimbabwe will accept only milled products that can't be planted and intermingled with native crops.

The 25-nation European Union last week ended a six-year moratorium against biotech food by allowing imports of one strain of processed sweet corn that can't be planted. Virtually all other biotech foods are still banned.

Agricultural giant Monsanto shelved plans on May 10 to introduce the world's first genetically engineered wheat, bowing to the worries of U.S. and Canadian farmers that Europe and Japan would reject all North American wheat imports.

Critics say biotech foods could spread allergens and toxins, and little is known about long-term safety issues. Fanatical opponents vow to destroy fields where the crops are grown and shut down a biotech conference in San Francisco in June.

Biotech food isn't a panacea, and its use need not race ahead of reasonable safety testing. But it could significantly improve the lives of billions. Groundless fears shouldn't be allowed to stand in the way.

VI. FOOD STAMPS AND FARM SUBSIDIES: HUNGER IN AMERICA

Editor's Introduction

The word "hunger" typically calls to mind images of arid farmland and frail children, but hunger does not always appear in such an obvious form. Hunger does not just mean famine, nor does it affect only developing countries. Citizens of industrialized nations suffer from hunger as well, albeit in a less pervasive, less malignant form. In America alone, approximately 33 million people are "food insecure," meaning they are not sure if they will be able to afford their next meal. Primarily low-income families hovering at or below the poverty line, the "food insecure" must rely on government aid to ensure having food on the table. Food stamps are the largest federal food program, with approximately $22 billion a year in funding; the program's bureaucracy, however, disqualifies many of those in need and discourages many of the families who do qualify. When food stamps are not an adequate or possible solution, food pantries present another option, but their supply—often composed of donations of old, damaged, or unpopular products from supermarkets and manufacturers—is dwindling as donors become more savvy about their inventory. This chapter asks how, in one of the richest countries in the world, there are still people who do not have enough to eat, and also looks at what can be and is being done to solve the problem.

In the chapter's first article, "Hungry in America," Trudy Lieberman reviews the history of hunger in the United States and examines current government reaction to the problem. Hunger has always existed in America, Lieberman says, but with poverty on the rise and government aid in decline, malnutrition is at its worst domestic level since the 1960s. Ultimately, Lieberman looks to Washington, D.C., for a solution, arguing that no modern industrialized nation, and particularly no nation as wealthy as the United States, should have a level of poverty that forces its citizens to use services such as food stamps and food pantries in the first place.

City Harvest, which Anna Quindlen profiles in "America's Hunger Epidemic," is one example of the many ways to approach the problem of hunger. The 25-year-old, New York–based group collects food from the city's restaurants and distributes it to the city's soup kitchens and shelters. Though she briefly discusses the government's role in alleviating hunger, Quindlen focuses on Americans' responsibility to help their fellow citizens.

One of the main reasons hunger persists in America has been the unwillingness on the part of Congress to fund aid programs in the short-term, and a refusal, until recently, to raise the minimum wage and help low-income families out of poverty in the long-term. A 2007 study, reported by Cheryl Wetzstein in "Cost of Hunger Calculated at $90 Billion," considers the societal costs of hunger in the United States, which can include mental health problems, high school dropouts, and absenteeism from work.

In the following article, "No Longer Hungry, Just Folks of 'Low Food Security,'" Marie Cocco explains the U.S. Department of Agriculture's controversial decision to change the terminology used to refer to the problem of hunger in the United States. Previously described as "food insecure, with hunger" or "food insecure, without hunger," Americans without a steady supply of food became, in the new rhetoric, people with "very low food security." With the change coming right before the 2006 Thanksgiving holiday, a time that revolves around food and feasting, the decision was widely criticized and viewed as representative of the government's insensitivity to and ignorance about domestic hunger.

Some members of government, however, know what it feels like to be dependent on food stamps—at least for a week. In "Lawmaker Cuts Budget to $3 a Day," Bella English follows U.S. Representative James P. McGovern (D-Mass.) as he participates in the Congressional Food Stamp Challenge, during which some members of the U.S. Congress subsisted for a week in 2007 on only government-allotted aid in order to draw attention to the need to increase funding for the food stamp program. Though the challenge was criticized by some, who argued that food stamps are intended to supplement one's diet rather than fully provide it, the participants received a great deal of media coverage by showing exactly what one can eat for approximately $3 a day (a banana, a bowl of lentils, and a tortilla with cheese, in one instance).

Hungry in America

By Trudy Lieberman
The Nation, August 18–25, 2003

I have no heart for somebody who starves his folks.

—George W. Bush discussing North Korean leader Kim Jong Il and US food donations on CNN (January 2, 2003)

Ellen Spearman lives in a trailer at the edge of Morrill, Nebraska, a tiny dusty town near the Wyoming state line. A few years ago she was a member of the working poor, earning $9.10 an hour at a local energy company. Then she got sick and had four surgeries for what turned out to be a benign facial tumor. New owners took over the company and told her she was a medical liability and could not work full time with benefits. For a while she worked part time without benefits until the company eliminated her position. So the 49-year-old single mother of five, with two teenage boys still at home, now lives on $21,300 a year from Social Security disability, child support and payments from the company's long-term disability policy she got as a benefit when she was first hired. That's about $6,000 above the federal poverty level, and too high to qualify for food stamps. But it is not enough to feed her family.

Food is the expendable item in a poor person's budget. With the need to pay for gasoline, car insurance, trailer rent, clothes, medicine and utilities, and to make payments on a car loan and $10,000 in medical bills, Spearman says three meals a day "take a back seat." She says she and her family eat a lot of rice with biscuits and gravy. Their diet is more interesting only when a local supermarket sells eight pieces of chicken for $3.99 or chuck roast for $1.49 a pound. "This country doesn't want to admit there's poverty," she says. "We can feed the world but not our own."

Spearman's predicament mirrors that of many Americans. While the most severe forms of malnutrition and starvation that prevailed through the 1960s have largely disappeared, some 33 million people live in households that aren't sure where their next meals are coming from—those whom policy analysts call the food insecure. And with poverty on the rise—the United States experienced the biggest jump in poverty in a decade in 2001, to nearly 12 percent of the population—their ranks are growing. At the end of 2002 the US Conference of Mayors reported a 19 percent increase in the demand for emergency food over the previous year. Food pantries, shelters, soup kitchens and other emergency food providers now serve at least 23 million people a year. "They are America's dirty little secret," says Larry Brown, who directs Brandeis University's Center on Hunger and Poverty. "They are hardworking have-nots who cannot pay the rent, medical bills, and still feed their families."

> Food and hunger are a lens through which we see what America has become.

Food and hunger are a lens through which we see what America has become: a country indifferent to the basic needs of its citizens, one that forces millions of them to rely on private charity that is inadequate, inefficient and frequently unavailable. As people with low and middle incomes have lost their jobs, their families line up for handouts, something many thought they'd never have to do. Hunger exposes the casualties of the ever-widening income gap between the rich and the rest of the population, and the damage inflicted by a twenty-year campaign waged by right-wing think tanks and conservative politicians to defund and delegitimize government. That campaign, which has succeeded in returning the public's view of poverty to the Darwinian one that prevailed before the Progressive Era at the turn of the twentieth century, is emblematic of the right's assault on public programs, which has used the old-fashioned notion of personal failing as the vehicle for accomplishing its political goals. Indeed, few politicians now advocate for the hungry.

The Way We Were

Beginning in the 1930s and into the 1940s, when Franklin Roosevelt articulated his Four Freedoms, including the freedom from want, America made a commitment, if not always perfectly executed, to feed the less fortunate. To be sure, the commitment was to some extent self-serving, in that food programs were designed to use up the surpluses produced by American agriculture. Still, there was a recognition that people couldn't always help themselves, and over the following decades champions emerged in Congress to battle for the needs of hungry people. From Robert Kennedy etching the face of hungry kids into the American conscience during his widely publicized trips to Appalachia to George McGovern and Bob Dole fighting for food stamps on the floor of the Senate, politicians stood up to help the hungry, putting government resources behind school lunches; school breakfasts; WIC, which feeds pregnant women and young children; and child nutrition.

When the nutrition programs under the Older Americans Act were created in 1972, authorizing special food programs for the elderly, it was Richard Nixon who pushed for more funding. Throughout the 1970s few Americans would have disputed the idea that the federal government had a major role to play in feeding the hungry. "Hunger was a problem we came much closer to solving in the 1970s," says

James Weill, president of the Food Research and Action Center. "Food stamps were more available, wages at the bottom were higher and there was less inequality."

But then came the Reagan Revolution, with its emphasis on cutting government and the taxes needed to support it. In 1981, when the Heritage Foundation published its first *Mandate for Leadership*, the right laid out its plan "to restrain the food programs" and reduce the federal government's role. Some of its proposals, like moving the functions of the Community Food and Nutrition Program to the states through block grants, have come to pass. That has meant less money, intensive competition among nonprofit organizations and ultimately less outreach and advocacy for the hungry.

In his speech accepting the Republican presidential nomination, Ronald Reagan coined the term "safety net." Implicit was the idea that like a trapeze artist who needed a safety net only to prevent rare catastrophes, government would help only those in dire need and that most of the time people could provide for themselves. Almost everyone, including many liberals, bought into the concept, which subtly shifted the purpose of social programs from assuring adequate living standards for all to helping the few who occasionally fell on hard times. Reagan attacked the legitimacy of food stamps by painting a picture of undeserving welfare queens who ate at the government trough while buying vodka with their benefits. That notion stuck, and public support for food programs waned.

Now conservatives are again on the attack. Last December in the *Washington Post* Outlook section, Douglas Besharov, director of the Project on Social and Individual Responsibility at the American Enterprise Institute, argued that the WIC program contributed to childhood obesity. He posited that real hunger is found "predominantly among people with behavioral or emotional problems such as drug addicts and the dysfunctional homeless," and he criticized liberal advocacy groups, unions and farmers for standing in the way of reform and modernization, code words the right often uses to build support for dismantling a program while making it seem like they're improving it. Conservative columnists and op-ed writers picked up his arguments. This year WIC and the child nutrition programs are scheduled for Congressional reauthorization. While there's no question Congress will reauthorize the programs, planting doubt about them increases the chance politicians will change the rules to make fewer people eligible. WIC is the golden child of the food programs. If it is tarnished, the rest will lose favor as well.

Less Money, Fewer Meals

Spending on the cluster of nine domestic food programs rose from $30.3 billion in 1982 to $42.7 billion in 1992 (in 2002 dollars). In the 2002 fiscal year it had fallen to $38.4 billion—less than 2 percent of the entire federal budget. Those numbers reflect drastic reductions over time—the Reagan Administration's cuts in 1981–82 and the cuts mandated by welfare reform in 1996—as well as modest funding increases between 1984 and 1993. "The cuts at the beginning of the Reagan Administration and the '96 cuts were far bigger than the modest increases in intervening years," says David Super, general counsel for the Center on Budget and Policy Priorities. "Funding has recovered partially but is well behind what it would have been had it not been for the cuts."

Food programs for the elderly have suffered a steep decline in federal appropriations after adjusting for inflation. In 2002 the government spent $716.5 million on home-delivered meals and on meals provided at senior centers. Ten years earlier it spent $767.4 million (in 2002 dollars), which explains why all over the country older Americans stay for months on waiting lists for a hot meal delivered to their door. The budget for New York City's home-delivered meals programs illustrates the federal government's fiscal retreat: Twenty years ago Washington funded 80 percent of the program and the city funded the rest. Today the federal government provides less than 20 percent, and city and private sources provide the balance.

Because food stamps are an entitlement, spending depends on how many people apply. Currently, that amount is about $22 billion, making food stamps by far the largest federal food program. Food stamps, which date back to 1939, have never been used by 100 percent of all people who are eligible. The high point came in 1994, when 75 percent of all eligible people were on the rolls; the low point was in 1999, when only 58 percent were getting help. "A golden era for the food-stamp program never existed," said Doug O'Brien, vice president of America's Second Harvest. There was a time, though, when government agencies, such as the now-defunct Community Services Administration, sponsored extensive outreach and advocacy programs with the goal of enrolling more people. But after the Heritage Foundation attacked its advocacy work in the early 1980s, enrolling more participants was no longer encouraged, remembers Charles Bell, a VISTA worker at the time.

Participation also depends on how hard states make the application process, and in the 1990s they made it very hard. Unfriendly rules requiring excessive verification, more frequent visits from caseworkers and the need to reapply in person, as well as pressure on the states to reduce their error rates, discouraged many from applying. California, New York and Texas have practically criminalized the process by requiring applicants to be fingerprinted, an action that automatically brands them as potential cheaters. It's hardly surprising that only about half of all eligible residents in those states get food stamps. Receiving food stamps has always carried a stigma—"It's an intentional thing that keeps the program small and saves money," says Agnes Molnar, a senior fellow at New York City's Community Food Resource Center. Food-stamp participation is rising again nationwide, but many states still discourage applicants. In New York City, despite a sharp increase in unemployment, food-stamp use actually dropped between 2001 and 2003. "Low-income people have walked away from the program," O'Brien says.

According to Mathematica Policy Research, the average monthly benefit is $185, but the actual amount varies by family size. For elderly people living alone the average bene-

---
Emergency food is now entrenched in nearly every city and town.

---

fit is $50, but for 35 percent of this group, the benefit is only $10 because medical expenses and rent are not high enough to offset their monthly income, usually less than $600 from Social Security's Supplemental Security Income. When Congress reauthorized the food-stamp program last year, a move to increase the minimum benefit to $25 failed. "Because of the obsolescence of the assumptions on which food-stamp levels are based, they are no longer sufficient to prevent or guarantee against hunger," says Janet Poppendieck, a sociology professor at Hunter College in New York City. The food-stamp program assumed that families had 30 percent of their income to spend on food, an estimation that was more realistic when there was a much larger supply of low-income housing. Food stamps were intended to fill in the gap between the 30 percent and the cost of an arbitrarily set thrifty food plan. But today poor families use 50–80 percent of their income on housing and have far less to spend on food. The food stamps they do get are not enough for an adequate diet. So families run out of food before the month ends. That's when they turn to the 50,000 food pantries and soup kitchens across the country, links in an intricate system of food rationing that began as a temporary response to cuts during the Reagan years.

Pantries as a Way of Life

Emergency food is now entrenched in nearly every city and town. It represents a fundamental failure of government to adequately feed its citizens. About 30 percent of the people who visit pantries receive food stamps—a stark indication that even those who do get stamps need more help and that many who need help are not getting them. The pantries' very existence lulls the public and politicians into believing they are the answer. But neither politicians nor anyone with adequate income would care to shop at them.

Food pantries are community supermarkets in poor neighborhoods. But shoppers can't come and go as they please, nor can they always choose the food they want. "Sometimes your heart can run away with your funds, especially when there are children involved," says Roy Lawton, a program director at Panhandle Community Services in western Nebraska. So, he adds, there must be limits. At his agency in Gering, people can come three times a year if they qualify. A family of four can have an income no greater than $23,920. If they have one dollar more, or if they've come too often, pantry workers send them to area churches that have less stringent rules.

The quantity of food people get is almost always restricted in some way. At Bread for the City in Washington, DC, workers simply hand clients a food bag after a computer check verifies that they have visited only once during the month. There's no choice of foods here. Food director Verneice Green explains that it would be "too chaotic" to let people in the back room, where the food is stored. At St. Paul of the Shipwreck in San Francisco, the pantry resembles a child's board game. At each stop along a room lined with shelves, a person can choose a set number of items according to a color code and family size. At the West Side Campaign Against Hunger in Manhattan, director Doreen Wohl wants her pantry to resemble a supermarket so clients feel better about taking handouts. The currency here are points assigned to each item. A four-person family can take ten points' worth of food from each of the protein, vegetable, fruit and dairy sections, while a two-person family is allotted six points. On a busy Wednesday 280 people wheel shopping carts through the aisles, but the shelves are not well-stocked. There was less emergency food from the federal government than Wohl had expected— 74,000 pounds less this year from the so-called TEFAP program.

At the pantries, people get hand-me-down food. It comes from supermarkets where it has stayed on the shelf too long or is damaged, or it comes from manufacturers that have produced too much of one item or made some product that didn't sell, like a cereal named Buzz Blasts or a soft drink that's blue. "Blueberry cola looks like windshield washer fluid, but in food banking, you take the good with the bad," says Bernie Beaudreau, director of the Rhode Island Community Food Bank. Castoff food, however, doesn't always make for the most nutritious diets, and arguably contributes to the diet-related health problems prevalent among the population forced to use food pantries. Amtrak has been a big supporter of the New England Shelter for Homeless Veterans in downtown Boston, and many of the 300,000 meals the shelter serves each year revolve around Italian wraps and sausage, egg and cheese breakfast sandwiches donated by Amtrak. "It's a struggle to provide a steady, nutritionally balanced diet, because of our reliance on donated food," says a shelter worker. Fresh meat and produce are often scarce at the pantries. Last fall in Lincoln, Nebraska, the Lincoln Action Program had enough ten-pound boxes of hamburger for the 400 to 600 people who were coming every week for food, and one day 300 clients lined up for onions, squash, apples and eggplant. But, says outreach worker Sheryl Haas, "there are weeks when the pickings are really slim."

They will grow slimmer as major changes sweep through the emergency food system. Many of the 216 food banks across the country that supply the pantries have less donated food to give away, particularly canned and boxed products that were once the food banks' staples. "Cereal donations are down 30–40 percent or more," says Frank Finnegan, who heads the St. Louis Area Food Bank. Mike Gillespie, who manages the warehouse for the Capital Area

Food Bank in Washington, DC, used to get a call once a month from Giant Food to pick up excess products, but now, he says, Giant hasn't called in months. In 2000 Giant gave the food bank about 2.5 million pounds of food. Last year its donation fell to 1.6 million pounds.

Ironically, food banks have caused supermarkets, manufacturers and restaurants to become aware of how much food they were giving away. With the help of scanning technology and just-in-time inventory systems, businesses changed their practices. At the same time, more outlets such as Super Wal-Marts, dollar stores and flea markets have sprung up where manufacturers can sell their products. Although they get tax breaks for donating, food companies would rather sell than donate.

The only bright spot is that more produce is available because food-bank managers have aggressively sought donations of fruit and vegetables, and major donors have given money so perishables can be shipped quickly around the country. Yet many pantries don't have adequate refrigeration, or they are staffed with elderly volunteers who can't lug around 100-pound bags of onions and potatoes.

Some food companies have embraced "cause marketing," a new kind of charity that ties a firm's brand with a warm, fuzzy cause like hunger. "It's doing well for the company and doing good at the same time," explains Carol Cone, CEO of Cone Communications in Boston. But cause marketing hardly begins to solve the needs of hungry people. With Cone's help, the giant ConAgra Foods supports some of the 900 Kids' Cafes around the country—including one of the twenty-eight in Washington, DC, that serve 1,200 kids out of 43,000 children who are eligible. Other individuals and groups try to fill in the gaps. Last year Washington Wizards owner Abe Pollin raised $1 million to pay for 680,000 meals during the summer, a time when supplies at food pantries run low and school breakfasts and lunches are not available. But when the money ran out, the meals stopped.

Underlying the premise of food banks was the notion that someday they would not be needed and would disappear. Instead, food banking has become big business. Pantries have proliferated, there are jobs to protect, salaries to pay, an infrastructure to maintain. Perhaps as a result, there's a split among food-bank leaders, with some believing they should advocate for government solutions to the fundamental problems of poverty and others believing that rounding up more donations is the answer. Some food-bank boards of directors are fearful of direct advocacy. "We've chosen not to get involved politically," says Finnegan. But, he says, "private industry is not going to be able to solve this problem. If it's anyone's responsibility, it's the government's."

Getting to Root Causes

Hunger, of course, is symptomatic of a deeper problem—inadequate income, which hits even the US military at a time when the country has chosen guns over butter. The WIC office located at

Offutt Air Force base near Omaha serves 650 servicewomen, wives of military personnel and their children each month. To qualify for free food, a family of three, for example, must have a gross income this year that's less than $28,231. "Most people don't have enough money. That's why they're in the program," says a WIC official. Through the years, however, feeding people through special programs rather than dealing with their lack of money became the palatable political choice.

Those who favor the route of special programs say it would not take a lot of money to insure that all Americans are fed. "Six billion dollars more could cut hunger in half in two years," says David Beckmann, president of Bread for the World. "It's an eminently solvable problem." But more government money is not likely. In fact, there will probably be less. Earlier this year House Republicans passed legislation that would transform the food-stamp program into a block grant, yet another way of pushing responsibility to the states and letting them decide when and if they have sufficient revenues to feed people. It's a way of converting an entitlement

---

Those who favor the route of special programs say it would not take a lot of money to insure that all Americans are fed.

---

into revenue streams for states. After a few years they can divert money to other programs. It's not hard to imagine what will happen to the needy if the recession and budget deficits continue for several years. At the same time, the Agriculture Department hopes to make it more difficult to qualify for free and reduced-price school lunches, because, it says, some kids are getting cheap lunches even though their families are not eligible. Data, however, show that when more income documentation is required, it reduces participation among eligible children.

Today it's hard to find a champion for the hungry in Congress, much less in the executive branch. Hunger is not seen as a pressing political problem. In January, representatives of food advocacy groups met with Agriculture Secretary Ann Veneman and were told there were no extra dollars for food. "We were told it's going to be a tight budget year," says Beckmann. "They said there would be no more money for child nutrition, and we had to think about how to do more with the money we've got." Robert Blancato, a food-advocacy group lobbyist, says food programs must be recast to generate Congressional interest. "In this environment, programs need additional buzzwords to survive," he says. "If you can repackage the meal programs so they don't look like meal programs, they have a better chance. There's a whole new priority structure in where the money is going."

Meanwhile, no one in Washington talks much about living wages, increasing the minimum wage, indexing it for inflation or expanding the earned-income tax credit. But living wages are the only solution if people are ever to move toward the self-sufficiency and personal responsibility that politicians and the public demand of them. It's hard to buy food when the money you have goes for ever-increasing shelter costs, healthcare because you have no insurance and child-care because there are few low-cost options.

No modern industrial nation should protect the nutritional well-being of its citizens through handouts. But until an outraged public decides that hunger is unacceptable in the richest country in history, there will be more Ellen Spearmans asking why they cannot feed their families.

America's Hunger Epidemic

By Anna Quindlen
Newsweek, December 11, 2006

Alex Toro threads his big white truck through traffic, making the kind of pilgrimage New York City foodies live for. No stop at Le Bernardin today, the French fish restaurant that is routinely named one of the city's best, or Whole Foods, the Tiffany of supermarkets, although Toro has been to both. Instead he pulls up to the Sullivan Street Bakery as the smell of freshly baked bread spills out onto the pavement, then moves on to Hale and Hearty Soups, where today there's Italian lentil and pasta e fagiole. Then it's up to Balducci's for big bags of rolls.

That's one part of his daily route. The second is the eaters, not the eateries. A small church with a shelter, a large one with a food pantry in the basement. At Holy Apostles Soup Kitchen the line snakes down the block, and the people on it look like the cast of one of those movies in which every variation of humanity is assembled in one place: young bike messengers, old alcoholics and a woman with silver hair and a good leather purse whose posture bespeaks fierce pride. One of the men calls out to Alex in a sandpaper voice, "You bring the bread?"

Nearly 25 years ago a simple and elegant Robin Hood of an idea took root in a fledgling organization called City Harvest. Take the overflow from New York's restaurants, hotels, wholesalers and markets, and pass it on to the soup kitchens, shelters and food pantries. This year the group expects to distribute more than 21 million pounds of food. Sad to say, New Yorkers need it.

At this time of year, as every lifestyle magazine seems to veer from the perfect cookie recipe to the surefire post-holiday diet, it's worth noting that the United States is still in the grip of a hunger epidemic. The Department of Agriculture released the figures just before most of us dug into our turkey and yams: 35 million people don't have enough food, 12 million of them children. America's Second Harvest, a consortium of emergency food organizations, says 25 million people sought help from it last year.

When a social problem is intractable and profoundly serious, you can usually complain that the public doesn't know, corporations don't care and philanthropy hasn't stepped up, that there's no creative thinking and limited resources. None of that is true of hunger in America. The resources exist: "There's food that we can pick up this hour that can be feeding people in the next hour, or be in the garbage by the end of the day," says Jennifer McLean, City Harvest's vice president of program operations. And Americans know real need exists, too; one survey showed that a majority of those polled believe hunger is as bad or worse here as in other developed countries.

Many companies have contributed manpower and money to the effort. Food banks have sprung up throughout the country. And some of the newest initiatives are plenty smart, like the school program that sends kids home for the weekend with a backpack full of food. Smart, and sad: the idea came in part because teachers who oversaw meal programs noticed how many kids gorged themselves on Fridays, preparing for two days of bare cupboards.

Even government can't take all the blame for some of the holes in this terribly porous safety net. A fraction of the students who eat subsidized school lunches also take part in breakfast programs, in part because schools have struggled with the logistics. That shortfall has left billions in federal subsidies unspent. And food banks report that only about a third of their patrons receive food stamps, although many more are eligible.

> In the short term treating symptoms works just fine for someone who has an empty stomach and an empty fridge.

Of course, applying for food stamps is an arduous process—in Nebraska the application runs 25 pages, and looking at the regulations made my head spin—and the offices at which to do so are open only during work hours, when the working poor have to be at work. And the USDA didn't inspire confidence when it decided for official purposes to replace the word "hunger" with something called "food security." Yeah, and ketchup is a vegetable.

Sometimes advocates complain that organizations like City Harvest are treating only the symptoms, not the underlying root causes. And some of those root causes are clear. It should be possible to apply for food stamps online and at off-hours. More schools should offer breakfast. And working people, who account for about a third of those who use emergency food programs, should be paid a living wage. The current minimum wage is a joke if you look at the cost of a loaf of bread.

But in the short term treating symptoms works just fine for someone who has an empty stomach and an empty fridge. In the back of Alex Toro's truck are bags of potatoes, cases of lemonade, flats of mayonnaise. Jilly Stephens, the executive director of City Harvest, has seen what happens after the truck arrives when she goes out in the field: the bowls, the spoons, the open mouths, the sated looks. Recently at one shelter she saw a brace of high chairs, neatly stacked, waiting for their tiny occupants. That's not food insecurity; that's unconscionable.

Cost of Hunger Calculated at $90 Billion

BY CHERYL WETZSTEIN
THE WASHINGTON TIMES, JUNE 5, 2007

Hunger in America leads to $90 billion a year in societal costs, such as mental-health problems that may arise when people miss too many meals, a study says.

"We realize that there are some 35 million people in our country that are at risk of hunger or going hungry every day," said Stephen J. Brady, president of Sodexho Foundation, which commissioned the report, "The Economic Cost of Domestic Hunger."

"It's important to inform the public debate and help the public understand that fact and put it into terms that are meaningful," he said.

The report estimates that the nation spends $14.5 billion a year on charitable anti-hunger efforts, such as food banks, local feeding programs and volunteer expenses. It also calculates that $66.8 billion is spent each year fighting depression, anxiety and other aspects of poor health that can accompany food insecurity, as well as $9.2 billion caused by hunger-related school dropouts and absenteeism at work.

The report concludes that boosting anti-hunger spending by an additional $10 billion to $12 billion a year is cost-effective and could even "virtually end hunger" in America.

"We ought to debate this," said J. Larry Brown, founding director of the Center on Hunger and Poverty at Brandeis University and lead author of the report, "because if we're right, we're spending far more by letting hunger exist than it would cost to end it."

The reported $90 billion cost burden does not include major public nutrition programs. According to the U.S. Department of Agriculture, federal spending on food-assistance programs totaled nearly $53 billion in fiscal 2006, a 4 percent increase from the previous year and the sixth year in a row that spending rose. The food-stamp program, which served nearly 27 million people in 2006, accounted for $33 billion in federal spending.

Robert Rector, senior research fellow for domestic policy at the Heritage Foundation, said the Sodexho report "detracts" rather than adds to understanding and that "there is no significant long-term hunger in this country."

"The principal nutrition-related health problem facing poor Americans is obesity," he said. "Families that are in chaos and turmoil will have temporary food shortages, along with hundreds of other problems. It does not mean that the food shortage is the principal cause of everything that's wrong in the family."

The food-stamp program is up for renewal this year and several politicians, including Oregon Gov. Theodore R. Kulongoski and Rep. Jim McGovern of Massachusetts, both Democrats, have highlighted the need for increased anti-hunger spending by attempting to live on $3-a-day food-stamp allotments. Critics have chided the politicians, noting that food stamps are intended to augment—not comprise—a family's normal food budget.

No Longer Hungry, Just Folks of "Low Food Security"

BY MARIE COCCO
THE RECORD (BERGEN COUNTY, N.J.), NOVEMBER 27, 2006

It hasn't the zesty political punch of that Reagan-era effort to turn ketchup into a vegetable. But really, could there be a more unfortunate time for the Agriculture Department to banish the word "hunger" from its description of people who are, well, hungry?

Just a week before most of America sat down for that excessive meal we call the Thanksgiving feast (second- and third-day snacking while watching football is optional), came a new definition for the millions among us who are more likely to turn up at a food pantry than at a well-set dining table.

They are now to be known as people with "very low food security."

They were previously known as "food insecure, with hunger." Those who had some, but not much, more to eat were known as "food insecure, without hunger." Now they're just suffering from "low food security."

The linguistic legerdemain doesn't change the method the USDA uses to count Americans—it says there are about 35.1 million—who are uncertain of having enough food or simply don't have enough money to buy it. The number of people without sufficient resources to get food has been climbing for five years, but leveled off in the latest survey, the department says.

Those Worst Off

But the worst-off households fared worse, with the number of people described as having "very low food security" climbing from 10.7 million to 10.8 million. These are households in which "the food intake of some household members was reduced and their normal eating patterns were disrupted," because they couldn't buy food.

In a word, they went hungry.

The switch of bureaucratic jargon came about after the White House budget office questioned why the agriculture researchers actually called hungry people "hungry." The USDA bucked the question to the National Academies of Science, where it was determined that using the word "hunger" wasn't entirely accurate, since the agriculture researchers can count people who say they don't have enough food—but can't necessarily describe the symptoms they experience while doing without.

Statistics just can't capture what it feels like to have a hollow pit in the stomach, to lose weight or get sick because of malnutrition.

The new wording doesn't seem malicious. But it does raise a meaningful question: Why are more than 35 million Americans going without food, or without enough of it?

About half of people who turned to a charitable food pantry last year already were living in households that received federal food stamps, the USDA's annual survey says. An even greater proportion—66 percent of those who turned to pantries—received at least some form of federal food assistance, including school lunches and the feeding program for women, infants and children.

"It's a 10-year story," says Jim Weill, president of the Food Research and Action Center. The 1996 welfare overhaul threw millions of legal immigrants and able-bodied adults without children out of the food stamp program. Though Congress restored eligibility little by little, it neglected to alter the program in ways that would stretch food-assistance dollars far enough to keep up with the economic changes buffeting low-income people.

Food stamp allotments assume that a family spends at least some of its own money on food. But depressed and stagnant wages for unskilled workers, coupled with astronomical rents, now leave them without the cash the government assumes they'll have to feed themselves. The average food stamp benefit allows $1 per person, per meal, according to Dottie Rosenbaum, a food assistance expert at the Center on Budget and Policy Priorities. "They don't have . . . other income to purchase food," Rosenbaum says. "Their food stamps may run out two weeks into the month."

> Statistics just can't capture what it feels like to have a hollow pit in the stomach, to lose weight or get sick because of malnutrition.

Missions Impossible

And when was the last time you made homemade chickpea dip? The market-basket of items the government uses to determine how much it costs a food stamp recipient to make "thrifty" foods relies heavily on the purchase of raw ingredients such as beans, which are then to be miraculously transformed into meals made from scratch. It's a feat few middle-class families can accomplish these days. For most food stamp recipients—the disabled, the elderly and low-wage workers with long and sometimes unpredictable hours—it's mission impossible.

So the public-relations gaffe the USDA made just as the holiday season was beginning could turn out to be more of a blessing than a bungle. Congress is due to reauthorize the food stamp program next year—a task that would usually draw little attention.

Now we know the problem isn't really what we call those who are hungry. It's finding a better way to feed them.

Lawmaker Cuts Budget to $3 a Day

By Bella English
The Boston Globe, May 19, 2007

US Representative James P. McGovern pushed his grocery cart along the aisle at Safeway in southeast D.C., pausing for an agonizing moment in front of the coffee. Safeway brand, the cheapest, is three bucks a can. "This gets my juices running in the morning," he said. Into the cart it went.

And out of the cart it came. He decided he could not afford it. Instead he headed for dairy, where he selected a large package of shredded cheese, on special for $3.50. It would help stretch his meals for the week.

Normally when he shops at Safeway, McGovern, 47 and a Worcester Democrat, throws things into the cart regardless of price. He is not a food stamp recipient who shops deliberately, mindful of every nickel. Except for this week.

From breakfast last Tuesday morning (a banana and tap water) to dinner Monday night (whatever he has left), the Democrat from Worcester is eating on a total of $21, or $1 per meal. Nationally, the average monthly food stamp benefit in fiscal 2005 was $94.05, or about $3 a day, according to the US Department of Agriculture. (It ranged geographically from $76.39 in Wisconsin to $163.85 in the US territory of Guam.)

McGovern's point is that the allocation is inadequate and forces the poor to make impossible choices among food, rent, heat, gasoline, and healthcare. He and Jo Ann Emerson, a Missouri Republican, cochair the House Hunger Caucus and are trying to raise awareness among their brethren and the public as the Farm Bill comes up for reauthorization this summer. The food stamp program is included in the bill, and the duo has asked that $4 billion be added to the current $33 billion budget that covered 26 million recipients last year, 430,000 of them in Massachusetts. Under the bill, a family of four would get an additional $48 a month.

"We want to urge or shame Congress into doing the right thing," McGovern said as he entered the Safeway market. "Thirty-six million people are what is called 'food insecure.' That's something we should all be ashamed of in the richest country in the world."

McGovern is a big guy: 6 feet, 188 pounds. He has a healthy appetite. He loves red wine and desserts. Every day he gets a candy bar from the vending machine. "I love food," he said. "Everything."

At Safeway, he was joined by his wife Lisa, who is also taking the challenge. Together they had $42 to spend. (Their two young children will not be on the food stamp diet.)

They were accompanied by expert shopper Toinette Wilson, a single mother of three on food stamps who is earning a cosmetology license. Wilson offered tips: Buy bags of pasta, rice, and frozen vegetables.

The McGoverns bypassed chicken breasts and got a cut-up chicken for $7.32. They skipped the lean ground beef they usually buy for a cheaper, fattier cut.

Should they get the bag of brown rice for $2.79 or the white for $2.19? They splurged on the brown. Should they buy butter? No, they could not afford it.

Then there's the coffee question. He wanted it but felt guilty. She encouraged him: "If you're going to be miserable all week . . ."

In the end, it was McGovern staff member Michael Mershon who saved the day by putting a small packet in the cart for $1.55.

Lisa headed for the checkout line while her husband dashed off with another cart for their last supper that night before their lean cuisine begins the next morning. He bought steaks, asparagus, tomatoes, and a bottle of pinot noir.

At the register, the total for the week comes to $41.70—30 cents under their food stamp allotment.

The total for that night's dinner for them and their two children: $44.

At home in southeast Washington, he broiled the steaks, sauteed the asparagus, and sliced the tomatoes.

The next morning, McGovern rose at 5 a.m.—it's usually 6:20—to soak and boil lentils. He also made bacon and eggs for Patrick, 9, and Molly, 5, and packed a banana for breakfast and a bowl of lentils for lunch.

That night he was off to speak at a National Immigration Forum dinner at the posh Mayflower hotel. "No, thank you," he said, as waiters offered trays of endive with goat cheese and asparagus wrapped in phyllo. At the open bar, he asked for tap water.

Dinner was difficult: The tables bore baskets of rolls and trays of petite pastries. He waved off a waiter and glumly unwrapped a cheese tortilla Lisa brought him: It was gone in four gulps.

Wednesday: McGovern attended a breakfast fund-raiser in his honor at Bistro Bis in the Hotel George. While others ate eggs, bacon, potatoes, and sweet rolls, and drink freshly squeezed orange juice and "great-smelling coffee," he had a banana and water. At lunch he traded his lentils for Jo Ann Emerson's chicken salad, a good deal for him. At dinner he attended a Hillary Clinton fund-raiser at the Georgetown home of Elizabeth and Smith Bagley. The guests, except for McGovern, nibbled on duck and spring rolls, and then dined on soup, ravioli, crab cakes, chicken, and various breads and desserts. He ate nothing until, back at his office, the chicken and rice he brought from home that morning. ("The chicken was OK. The rice was gross—soggy and cold.")

Walking home from his office at 9:30, he ran into several colleagues sitting out at sidewalk cafes. Would he join them, several asked. He wanted to, but declined. One friend jokingly inquired whether he would be sleeping on a grate that night.

Thursday: It was a banana again for breakfast. He and Lisa talked about how in the scheme of life, this week's menu was just a minor inconvenience. "We know that on Tuesday we can go crazy and eat whatever we want," he said. "Doing this week after week after week must be just awful."

He prepared his lunch: lentils and "a tiny chicken wing." In the evening, he attended an Oxfam America reception, skipping the hors d'oeuvres, and gave a speech about world hunger. Later, Lisa and the children brought dinner to his office: spaghetti made with the hamburger and a jar of tomato sauce.

Yesterday: McGovern wolfed the last banana for breakfast, chasing it with water. He was hoarding his packet of coffee for the weekend, which he expected to be particularly hard: more free time, little food left.

Lunch was leftover pasta; dinner was scrambled eggs with potato and cheese. He had lost three pounds in four days.

But he felt his forced diet had done some good. "Our point in doing this was to get attention, to get people talking, and to raise awareness," he said. "It was also for us to learn. That's happening."

Tuesday, when they're back to their old lives, Lisa will reach first for a Diet Coke. He's thinking of a "nice, grilled New York strip." And all the coffee he wants.

APPENDIX

United Nations Millennium Declaration

UNITED NATIONS GENERAL ASSEMBLY, SEPTEMBER 18, 2000

Fifty-fifth session
Agenda item 60 (b)
00 55951

Resolution adopted by the General Assembly

[without reference to a Main Committee (A/55/L.2)]
55/2. United Nations Millennium Declaration

The General Assembly
Adopts the following Declaration:

United Nations Millennium Declaration

I. Values and principles

1. We, heads of State and Government, have gathered at United Nations Headquarters in New York from 6 to 8 September 2000, at the dawn of a new millennium, to reaffirm our faith in the Organization and its Charter as indispensable foundations of a more peaceful, prosperous and just world.

2. We recognize that, in addition to our separate responsibilities to our individual societies, we have a collective responsibility to uphold the principles of human dignity, equality and equity at the global level. As leaders we have a duty therefore to all the world's people, especially the most vulnerable and, in particular, the children of the world, to whom the future belongs.

3. We reaffirm our commitment to the purposes and principles of the Charter of the United Nations, which have proved timeless and universal. Indeed, their relevance and capacity to inspire have increased, as nations and peoples have become increasingly interconnected and interdependent.

4. We are determined to establish a just and lasting peace all over the world in accordance with the purposes and principles of the Charter. We rededicate ourselves to support all efforts to uphold the sovereign equality of all States, respect for their territorial integrity and political independence, resolution of disputes by peaceful means and in conformity with the principles of justice and international law, the right to self-determination of peoples which remain under colonial domination and foreign occupation, non-interference in the internal affairs of States, respect for human rights and fundamental freedoms, respect for the equal rights of all without distinction as to race, sex, language or religion and international cooperation in solving international problems of an economic, social, cultural or humanitarian character.

5. We believe that the central challenge we face today is to ensure that globalization becomes a positive force for all the world's people. For while globalization offers great opportunities, at present its benefits are very unevenly shared, while its costs are unevenly distributed. We recognize that developing countries and countries with economies in transition face special difficulties in responding to this central challenge. Thus, only through broad and sustained efforts to create a shared future, based upon our common humanity in all its diversity, can globalization be made fully inclusive and equitable. These efforts must include policies and measures, at the global level, which correspond to the needs of developing countries and economies in transition and are formulated and implemented with their effective participation.

6. We consider certain fundamental values to be essential to international relations in the twenty-first century. These include:

- **Freedom**. Men and women have the right to live their lives and raise their children in dignity, free from hunger and from the fear of violence, oppression or injustice. Democratic and participatory governance based on the will of the people best assures these rights.

- **Equality.** No individual and no nation must be denied the opportunity to benefit from development. The equal rights and opportunities of women and men must be assured.

- **Solidarity.** Global challenges must be managed in a way that distributes the costs and burdens fairly in accordance with basic principles of equity and social justice. Those who suffer or who benefit least deserve help from those who benefit most.

- **Tolerance.** Human beings must respect one other, in all their diversity of belief, culture and language. Differences within and between societies should be neither feared nor repressed, but cherished as a precious asset of humanity. A culture of peace and dialogue among all civilizations should be actively promoted.

- **Respect for nature.** Prudence must be shown in the management of all living species and natural resources, in accordance with the precepts of sustainable development. Only in this way can the immeasurable riches provided to us by nature be preserved and passed on to our descendants. The current unsustainable patterns of production and consumption must be changed in the interest of our future welfare and that of our descendants.

- **Shared responsibility.** Responsibility for managing worldwide economic and social development, as well as threats to international peace and security, must be shared among the nations of the world and should be exercised multilaterally. As the most universal and most representative organization in the world, the United Nations must play the central role.

7. In order to translate these shared values into actions, we have identified key objectives to which we assign special significance.

II. Peace, security and disarmament

8. We will spare no effort to free our peoples from the scourge of war, whether within or between States, which has claimed more than 5 million lives in the past decade. We will also seek to eliminate the dangers posed by weapons of mass destruction.

9. We resolve therefore:

- To strengthen respect for the rule of law in international as in national affairs and, in particular, to ensure compliance by Member States with the decisions of the International Court of Justice, in compliance with the Charter of the United Nations, in cases to which they are parties.

- To make the United Nations more effective in maintaining peace and security by giving it the resources and tools it needs for conflict prevention, peaceful resolution of disputes, peacekeeping, post-conflict peace-building and reconstruction. In this context, we take note of the report of the Panel on United Nations Peace Operations[1] and request the General Assembly to consider its recommendations expeditiously.

- To strengthen cooperation between the United Nations and regional organizations, in accordance with the provisions of Chapter VIII of the Charter.

- To ensure the implementation, by States Parties, of treaties in areas such as arms control and disarmament and of international humanitarian law and human rights law, and call upon all States to consider signing and ratifying the Rome Statute of the International Criminal Court.[2]

- To take concerted action against international terrorism, and to accede as soon as possible to all the relevant international conventions.

- To redouble our efforts to implement our commitment to counter the world drug problem.

- To intensify our efforts to fight transnational crime in all its dimensions, including trafficking as well as smuggling in human beings and money laundering.

- To minimize the adverse effects of United Nations economic sanctions on innocent populations, to subject such sanctions regimes to regular reviews and to eliminate the adverse effects of sanctions on third parties.

- To strive for the elimination of weapons of mass destruction, particularly nuclear weapons, and to keep all options open for achieving this aim, including the possibility of convening an international conference to identify ways of eliminating nuclear dangers.

- To take concerted action to end illicit traffic in small arms and light weapons, especially by making arms transfers more transparent and supporting regional disarmament measures, taking account of all the recommendations of the forthcoming United Nations Conference on Illicit Trade in Small Arms and Light Weapons.

- To call on all States to consider acceding to the Convention on the Prohibition of the Use, Stockpiling, Production and Transfer of Anti-personnel Mines and on Their Destruction,[3] as well as the amended mines protocol to the Convention on conventional weapons.[4]

10. We urge Member States to observe the Olympic Truce, individually and collectively, now and in the future, and to support the International Olympic Committee in its efforts to promote peace and human understanding through sport and the Olympic Ideal.

III. Development and poverty eradication

11. We will spare no effort to free our fellow men, women and children from the abject and dehumanizing conditions of extreme poverty, to which more than a billion of them are currently subjected. We are committed to making the right to development a reality for everyone and to freeing the entire human race from want.

12. We resolve therefore to create an environment—at the national and global levels alike—which is conducive to development and to the elimination of poverty.

13. Success in meeting these objectives depends, *inter alia*, on good governance within each country. It also depends on good governance at the international level and on transparency in the financial, monetary and trading systems. We are committed to an open, equitable, rule-based, predictable and nondiscriminatory multilateral trading and financial system.

14. We are concerned about the obstacles developing countries face in mobilizing the resources needed to finance their sustained development. We will therefore make every effort to ensure the success of the High-level International and Intergovernmental Event on Financing for Development, to be held in 2001.

15. We also undertake to address the special needs of the least developed countries. In this context, we welcome the Third United Nations Conference on the Least Developed Countries to be held in May 2001 and will endeavour to ensure its success. We call on the industrialized countries:

- To adopt, preferably by the time of that Conference, a policy of duty- and quota-free access for essentially all exports from the least developed countries;

- To implement the enhanced programme of debt relief for the heavily indebted poor countries without further delay and to agree to cancel all official bilateral debts of those countries in return for their making demonstrable commitments to poverty reduction; and

- To grant more generous development assistance, especially to countries that are genuinely making an effort to apply their resources to poverty reduction.

16. We are also determined to deal comprehensively and effectively with the debt problems of low- and middle-income developing countries, through various national and international measures designed to make their debt sustainable in the long term.

17. We also resolve to address the special needs of small island developing States, by implementing the Barbados Programme of Action[5] and the outcome of the twenty-second special session of the General Assembly rapidly and in full. We urge the international community to ensure that, in the development of a vulnerability index, the special needs of small island developing States are taken into account.

18. We recognize the special needs and problems of the landlocked developing countries, and urge both bilateral and multilateral donors to increase financial and technical assistance to this group of countries to meet their special development needs and to help them overcome the impediments of geography by improving their transit transport systems.

19. We resolve further:

- To halve, by the year 2015, the proportion of the world's people whose income is less than one dollar a day and the proportion of people who suffer from hunger and, by the same date, to halve the proportion of people who are unable to reach or to afford safe drinking water.

- To ensure that, by the same date, children everywhere, boys and girls alike, will be able to complete a full course of primary schooling and that girls and boys will have equal access to all levels of education.

- By the same date, to have reduced maternal mortality by three quarters, and under-five child mortality by two thirds, of their current rates.

- To have, by then, halted, and begun to reverse, the spread of HIV/AIDS, the scourge of malaria and other major diseases that afflict humanity.

- To provide special assistance to children orphaned by HIV/AIDS.

- By 2020, to have achieved a significant improvement in the lives of at least 100 million slum dwellers as proposed in the "Cities Without Slums" initiative.

20. We also resolve:

- To promote gender equality and the empowerment of women as effective ways to combat poverty, hunger and disease and to stimulate development that is truly sustainable.

- To develop and implement strategies that give young people everywhere a real chance to find decent and productive work.

- To encourage the pharmaceutical industry to make essential drugs more widely available and affordable by all who need them in developing countries.

- To develop strong partnerships with the private sector and with civil society organizations in pursuit of development and poverty eradication.

- To ensure that the benefits of new technologies, especially information and communication technologies, in conformity with recommendations contained in the ECOSOC 2000 Ministerial Declaration,[6] are available to all.

IV. Protecting our common environment

21. We must spare no effort to free all of humanity, and above all our children and grandchildren, from the threat of living on a planet irredeemably spoilt by human activities, and whose resources would no longer be sufficient for their needs.

22. We reaffirm our support for the principles of sustainable development, including those set out in Agenda 21,[7] agreed upon at the United Nations Conference on Environment and Development.

23. We resolve therefore to adopt in all our environmental actions a new ethic of conservation and stewardship and, as first steps, we resolve:

- To make every effort to ensure the entry into force of the Kyoto Protocol, preferably by the tenth anniversary of the United Nations Conference on Environment and Development in 2002, and to embark on the required reduction in emissions of greenhouse gases.

- To intensify our collective efforts for the management, conservation and sustainable development of all types of forests.

- To press for the full implementation of the Convention on Biological Diversity[8] and the Convention to Combat Desertification in those Countries Experiencing Serious Drought and/or Desertification, particularly in Africa.[9]

- To stop the unsustainable exploitation of water resources by developing water management strategies at the regional, national and local levels, which promote both equitable access and adequate supplies.

- To intensify cooperation to reduce the number and effects of natural and man-made disasters.

- To ensure free access to information on the human genome sequence.

V. Human rights, democracy and good governance

24. We will spare no effort to promote democracy and strengthen the rule of law, as well as respect for all internationally recognized human rights and fundamental freedoms, including the right to development.

25. We resolve therefore:

- To respect fully and uphold the Universal Declaration of Human Rights.[10]

- To strive for the full protection and promotion in all our countries of civil, political, economic, social and cultural rights for all.

- To strengthen the capacity of all our countries to implement the principles and practices of democracy and respect for human rights, including minority rights.

- To combat all forms of violence against women and to implement the Convention on the Elimination of All Forms of Discrimination against Women.[11]

- To take measures to ensure respect for and protection of the human rights of migrants, migrant workers and their families, to eliminate the increasing acts of racism and xenophobia in many societies and to promote greater harmony and tolerance in all societies.

- To work collectively for more inclusive political processes, allowing genuine participation by all citizens in all our countries.

- To ensure the freedom of the media to perform their essential role and the right of the public to have access to information.

VI. Protecting the vulnerable

26. We will spare no effort to ensure that children and all civilian populations that suffer disproportionately the consequences of natural disasters, genocide, armed conflicts and other humanitarian emergencies are given every assistance and protection so that they can resume normal life as soon as possible.

We resolve therefore:

- To expand and strengthen the protection of civilians in complex emergencies, in conformity with international humanitarian law.

- To strengthen international cooperation, including burden sharing in, and the coordination of humanitarian assistance to, countries hosting refugees and to help all refugees and displaced persons to return voluntarily to their homes, in safety and dignity and to be smoothly reintegrated into their societies.

- To encourage the ratification and full implementation of the Convention on the Rights of the Child[12] and its optional protocols on the involvement of children in armed conflict and on the sale of children, child prostitution and child pornography.[13]

VII. Meeting the special needs of Africa

27. We will support the consolidation of democracy in Africa and assist Africans in their struggle for lasting peace, poverty eradication and sustainable development, thereby bringing Africa into the mainstream of the world economy.

28. We resolve therefore:

- To give full support to the political and institutional structures of emerging democracies in Africa.

- To encourage and sustain regional and subregional mechanisms for preventing conflict and promoting political stability, and to ensure a reliable flow of resources for peace-keeping operations on the continent.

- To take special measures to address the challenges of poverty eradication and sustainable development in Africa, including debt cancellation, improved market access, enhanced Official Development Assistance and increased flows of Foreign Direct Investment, as well as transfers of technology.

- To help Africa build up its capacity to tackle the spread of the HIV/AIDS pandemic and other infectious diseases.

VIII. Strengthening the United Nations

29. We will spare no effort to make the United Nations a more effective instrument for pursuing all of these priorities: the fight for development for all the peoples of the world, the fight against poverty, ignorance and disease; the fight against injustice; the fight against violence, terror and crime; and the fight against the degradation and destruction of our common home.

30. We resolve therefore:

- To reaffirm the central position of the General Assembly as the chief deliberative, policy-making and representative organ of the United Nations, and to enable it to play that role effectively.

- To intensify our efforts to achieve a comprehensive reform of the Security Council in all its aspects.

- To strengthen further the Economic and Social Council, building on its recent achievements, to help it fulfil the role ascribed to it in the Charter.

- To strengthen the International Court of Justice, in order to ensure justice and the rule of law in international affairs.

- To encourage regular consultations and coordination among the principal organs of the United Nations in pursuit of their functions.

- To ensure that the Organization is provided on a timely and predictable basis with the resources it needs to carry out its mandates.

- To urge the Secretariat to make the best use of those resources, in accordance with clear rules and procedures agreed by the General Assembly, in the interests of all Member States, by adopting the best management practices and technologies available and by concentrating on those tasks that reflect the agreed priorities of Member States.

- To promote adherence to the Convention on the Safety of United Nations and Associated Personnel.[14]

- To ensure greater policy coherence and better cooperation between the United Nations, its agencies, the Bretton Woods Institutions and the World Trade Organization, as well as other multilateral bodies, with a view to achieving a fully coordinated approach to the problems of peace and development.

- To strengthen further cooperation between the United Nations and national parliaments through their world organization, the Inter-Parliamentary Union, in various fields, including peace and security, economic and social development, international law and human rights and democracy and gender issues.

- To give greater opportunities to the private sector, non-governmental organizations and civil society, in general, to contribute to the realization of the Organization's goals and programmes.

31. We request the General Assembly to review on a regular basis the progress made in implementing the provisions of this Declaration, and ask the Secretary-General to issue periodic reports for consideration by the General Assembly and as a basis for further action.

32. We solemnly reaffirm, on this historic occasion, that the United Nations is the indispensable common house of the entire human family, through which we will seek to realize our universal aspirations for peace, cooperation and development. We therefore pledge our unstinting support for these common objectives and our determination to achieve them.

8th plenary meeting
8 September 2000

1 A/55/305-S/2000/809; see Official Records of the Security Council, Fifty-fifth Year, Supplement for July, August and September 2000, document S/2000/809.

2 A/CONF.183/9.

3 See CD/1478.

4 Amended protocol on prohibitions or restrictions on the use of mines, booby-traps and other devices (CCW/CONF.I/16 (Part I), annex B).

5 Programme of Action for the Sustainable Development of Small Island Developing States (Report of the Global Conference on the Sustainable Development of Small Island Developing States, Bridgetown, Barbados, 25 April-6 May 1994 (United Nations publication, Sales No. E.94.I.18 and corrigenda), chap. I, resolution 1, annex II).

6 E/2000/L.9.

7 Report of the United Nations Conference on Environment and Development, Rio de Janeiro, 3-14 June 1992 (United Nations publication, Sales No. E.93.I.8 and corrigenda), vol. I: Resolutions adopted by the Conference, resolution 1, annex II.

8 See United Nations Environment Programme, Convention on Biological Diversity (Environmental Law and Institution Programme Activity Centre), June 1992.

9 A/49/84/Add.2, annex, appendix II.

10 Resolution 217 A (III).

11 Resolution 34/180, annex.

12 Resolution 44/25, annex.

13 Resolution 54/263, annexes I and II.

14 Resolution 49/59, annex.

BIBLIOGRAPHY

Books

Ahmed, Raisuddin, Steven Haggblade, and Tawfiq-e-Elahi Chowdhury. *Out of the Shadow of Famine: Evolving Food Markets and Food Policy in Bangladesh*. Baltimore, Md.: Johns Hopkins University Press, 2000.

Aiken, William, and Hugh la Follette. *World Hunger and Morality*. 2nd ed. Upper Saddle River, N.J.: Prentice Hall, 1996.

Becker, Jasper. *Hungry Ghosts: Mao's Secret Famine*. New York: Henry Holt and Company, Inc., 1998.

Boucher, Douglas M., ed. *The Paradox of Plenty: Hunger in a Bountiful World*. Oakland, Cal.: Food First, 1999.

Cliggett, Lisa. *Grains from Grass: Aging, Gender, and Famine in Rural Africa*. Ithaca, N.Y.: Cornell University Press, 2005.

De Waal, Alex. *Famine Crimes: Politics & the Disaster Relief Industry in Africa*. Bloomington, Ind.: Indiana University Press, 1997.

———. *Famine That Kills: Darfur, Sudan*. Rev. ed. New York: Oxford University Press, 2004.

Downs, R. E., Donna O. Kerner, and Stephen P. Reyna, eds. *The Political Economy of African Famine*. Amsterdam: Gordon and Breach Science Publishers, 1993.

Dreze, Jean, Amartya Sen, and Athar Hussain, eds. *The Political Economy of Hunger*. New York: Oxford University Press, 1995.

Edwards, R. Dudley, and Thomas Desmond Williams, eds. *The Great Famine: Studies in Irish History, 1845–52*. Dublin: The Lilliput Press, 1999.

Eisinger, Peter K. *Toward an End to Hunger in America*. Washington, D.C.: The Brookings Institution, 1998.

Fogel, Robert W. *The Escape from Hunger and Premature Death, 1700–2100: Europe, America, and the Third World*. New York: Cambridge University Press, 2004.

Haggard, Stephan, and Marcus Noland. *Famine in North Korea: Markets, Aid, and Reform*. New York: Columbia University Press, 2007.

Hall, Tony. *Changing the Face of Hunger*. Nashville, Tenn.: Thomas Nelson, 2007.

Hesser, Leon. *The Man Who Fed the World: Nobel Peace Prize Laureate Norman Borlaug and His Battle to End World Hunger*. Dallas, Tex.: Durban House Publishing Company, Inc., 2006.

Jordan, William Chester. *The Great Famine: Northern Europe in the Early Fourteenth Century*. Princeton, N.J.: Princeton University Press, 1996.

Kaplan, Robert D. *Surrender or Starve: Travels in Ethiopia, Sudan, Somalia, and Eritrea*. New York: Vintage, 2003.

Kent, George, and Jean Ziegler. *Freedom from Want: The Human Right to Adequate Food*. Washington, D.C.: Georgetown University Press, 2005.

Lappe, Frances M., et al. *World Hunger: Twelve Myths.* New York: Grove Press, 1998.

Leisinger, Klaus M., Karin Schmitt, and Rajul Pandya-Lorch. *Six Billion and Counting: Population Growth and Food Security in the 21st Century.* Washington, D.C.: International Food Policy Research Institute, 2002.

McGovern, George. *The Third Freedom: Ending Hunger in Our Time.* New York: Simon & Schuster, 2002.

McGovern, George, Bob Dole, and Donald E. Messner. *Ending Hunger Now: A Challenge to Persons of Faith.* Minneapolis, Minn.: Augsburg Fortress, 2005.

Menzel, Peter, and Faith d'Aluisio. *Hungry Planet: What the World Eats.* Berkeley, Cal.: Ten Speed Press, 2005.

Moeller, Susan D. *Compassion Fatigue: How the Media Sell Disease, Famine, War and Death.* New York: Routledge, 1999.

Natsios, Andrew S. *The Great North Korean Famine: Famine, Politics, and Foreign Policy.* Washington, D.C.: Institute of Peace Press, 2002.

Ó'Gráda, Cormac. *Black '47 and Beyond: The Great Irish Famine in History, Economy, and Memory.* Princeton, N.J.: Princeton University Press, 1999.

Pinstrup-Anderson, Per, and Ebbe Schiøler. *Seeds of Contention: World Hunger and the Global Controversy over GM Crops.* Baltimore, Md.: Johns Hopkins University Press, 2000.

Pringle, Peter. *Food, Inc.: Mendel to Monsanto—The Promises and Perils of the Biotech Harvest.* New York: Simon & Schuster, 2003.

Runge, C. Ford, et al. *Ending Hunger in Our Lifetime: Food Security and Globalization.* Baltimore, Md.: Johns Hopkins University Press, 2003.

Russell, Sharman Apt. *Hunger: An Unnatural History.* New York: Basic Books, 2005.

Schwartz-Nobel, Loretta. *Growing Up Empty: How Federal Policies Are Starving America's Children.* New York: HarperCollins, 2003.

Seavoy, Ronald E. Famine in Peasant Societies. New York: Greenwood Press, 1986.

Shiva, Vandana. *Stolen Harvest: The Hijacking of the Global Food Supply.* Cambridge, Mass.: South End Press, 2000.

UN Millennium Project 2005. *Halving Hunger: It Can Be Done.* London: Earthscan, 2005.

United Nations World Food Programme. *World Hunger Series 2006: Hunger and Learning.* Palo Alto, Cal.: Stanford University Press, 2006.

Vaughan, Megan. *The Story of an African Famine: Gender and Famine in Twentieth-Century Malawi.* New York: Cambridge University Press, 1987.

Von Braun, Joachim, Tesfaye Teklu, and Patrick Webb. *Famine in Africa: Causes, Responses, and Prevention.* Baltimore, Md.: Johns Hopkins University Press, 1999.

Web Sites

Readers seeking additional information about world hunger may wish to refer to the following Web sites, all of which were operational as of this writing.

Feeding Minds, Feeding Hunger

www.feedingminds.org

Launched on World Food Day 2000, Feeding Minds, Feeding Hunger is a global education project designed to encourage teachers and young students to become involved in the fight against hunger. The Web site includes model lessons for teachers to help them educate their students about hunger.

Food and Agriculture Organization of the United Nations

www.fao.org

Founded in 1945, the Food and Agriculture Organization (FAO) of the United Nations serves as a neutral forum for both developed and developing nations to discuss food and agriculture policy. The FAO's Web site contains a number of statistical databases and articles relating to the management of agriculture, forestry, and fisheries.

International Food Policy Research Institute

www.ifpri.org

Part of the Consultative Group on International Agricultural Research, the International Food Policy Research Institute (IFPRI) seeks to develop policy solutions to address hunger in developing nations in a sustainable manner. The IFPRI's Web site presents its research and its current recommendations, primarily its 2020 Vision Initiative, which hopes to establish universal, sustainable food security by the year 2020.

Micronutrient Initiative

www.micronutrient.org

An international, not-for-profit organization, the Micronutrient Initiative aims to eliminate vitamin and mineral deficiencies universally. The Web site gives a detailed analysis of the micronutrient status of more than 70 countries.

United Nations World Food Programme

www.wfp.org

The World Food Programme (WFP) is the United Nations' "frontline agency in the fight against global hunger." Responsible for both emergency response and long-term projects, the WFP is currently working on the U.N. Millennium Development Goal of halving world hunger by 2015, frequently posting updates on its activities.

United Nations World Food Programme—Interactive Hunger Map
www.wfp.org/country_brief/hunger_map/map/hungermap_popup/ map_popup.html

A feature of the WFP's Web site, this interactive map allows the user to click on any region or country in the world to learn the area's population and the percentage of citizens who are undernourished. In many cases, the map also offers information on the causes of hunger and on the WFP's relief efforts in the specific region.

World Health Organization—Nutrition
www.who.int/nutrition

A section of the World Health Organization's larger Web site, this page on nutrition offers basic information on nutritional requirements, as well as descriptions of several types of malnutrition.

World Hunger Education Service (WHES)—Hunger Notes
www.worldhunger.org

The online publication of the World Hunger Education Service, Hunger Notes provides links to hunger-related stories in major international newspapers and news outlets.

Additional Periodical Articles with Abstracts

More information about world hunger and related subjects can be found in the following articles. Readers who require a more comprehensive selection are advised to consult the *Readers' Guide Abstracts* and other H. W. Wilson publications.

Fifty Years of U.S. Food Aid and Its Role in Reducing World Hunger. Shahla Shapouri and Stacey Rosen. *Amber Waves* v. 2 pp38–43 September 2004.

Shapouri and Rosen discuss the history and future of American food-aid programs. The actions of the United States have a profound effect on the actions of other food donors and on the system as a whole. The 50th anniversary of the American food aid program in 2004 is a good time to assess the program and reexamine plans; the American government is taking steps to develop transparent methods to monitor the effectiveness of food aid in reducing hunger in recipient countries. Lessons from the past could be useful in improving food aid's effectiveness: Emergency food aid has saved lives, but program food aid, or government-to-government donations that are usually sold in recipient country markets, has had mixed results.

Hunger USA. *America* v. 194 p5 April 24–May 1, 2006.

The U.S. Conference of Mayors' annual Hunger and Homelessness Survey indicates that hunger and food insecurity—not always having access to enough food to meet basic needs—not only exist in the United States but are on the rise, this article reports. The increase is reflected in the fact that the two dozen cities polled reported that requests for emergency food at pantries and similar sites had risen on average by 12 percent. Despite the nutritional benefits to low-income people who use the various federal food programs, President George W. Bush's fiscal year 2007 budget is proposing cuts that would reduce these benefits. Congress should firmly resist cutting back on federal nutrition programs and concentrate instead on bolstering them in such a way as to eliminate hunger and guarantee food security in the United States.

How the Other Half Eats. Rebecca Poynor Burns. *Atlanta Magazine* v. 42 pp97–103 March 2003.

A growing number of Atlantans are struggling to put food on the table, Burns observes. In 2002, requests to the food bank had increased by 30 percent. The increased demand came from working parents afflicted by high rents and stagnant pay, middle-income and white-collar families stricken by layoffs, senior citizens fighting to get by on fixed incomes, and single mothers who went off welfare and found themselves laid off and their pre–Welfare Reform safety nets taken away. Burns discusses various individuals and organizations that distribute food to the hungry.

Genetic Engineering, the Farm Crisis, and World Hunger. Carl F. Jordan. *BioScience* v. 52 pp523–29 June 2002.

The belief that genetic engineering can benefit the small farmer and alleviate world hunger has made it hard to grasp that genetically modified crops have already added to the financial crisis of U.S. farmers and increased the gap between rich and poor in developing nations, Jordan argues. Reluctance to challenge such notions has led to huge investments in genetic engineering to the neglect of other more promising but less glamorous strategies. In developing nations, new approaches could mean promoting rediscovery of local crop varieties that are ecologically and culturally adapted to local conditions. Moreover, small farmers in food-deprived countries could be urged to grow food for their families and neighbors instead of products to be sold overseas by the national government.

Hunger Pains. *Canada and the World Backgrounder* v. 69 pp18–20 September 2003.

Although there is enough food in the world for everybody, one out of every seven people worldwide goes hungry, the article says. Sending food to those hit by famine does not eradicate hunger and starvation in the long run. Food was shipped to Ethiopia in the 1980s, but the same famine conditions have recently reemerged. The problem is that 70 percent of the world's poor live in rural areas and depend solely on the crops they grow themselves, making them vulnerable to natural disasters, such as droughts and floods. These people require aid for development projects, including irrigation, to help prevent the next crisis.

As World Food Production Increases, So Does the Number of Hungry. Daniel Shepard. *Choices* v. 13 p28 March 2004.

The number of hungry is increasing despite the fact that the world is producing more food now than ever before, Shepard notes. Since the early 1970s, food production has tripled, yet approximately 800 million people in developing nations, or 18 percent of the world's population, suffer from hunger. Hunger is increasing in sub-Saharan Africa, where 183 million people, or one-third of the population, is considered undernourished, and hunger is also increasing in the world's cities, where the urban poor now constitute more than one-fifth of the hungry. This situation perpetuates poverty because it prevents people from reaching their potential and contributing to the progress of their societies.

Famine Again? Tim Stafford. *Christianity Today* v. 51 pp42–47 May 2007.

More needs to be done to permanently solve the perennial famines in the world's poorest countries, Stafford asserts. The problem of continuing hunger lies with those who have not joined or cannot join the modern economy—those in poverty-stricken urban slums, whose labor will not earn sufficient money to buy food, or those in remote places pursuing traditional lifestyles that are subject to natural disasters. To make a lasting difference, people in relief and development organizations must help people change their lives. Stafford describes a visit to Kenya to see the work that the aid agency World Vision is doing there.

Running on Empty. Nathan Lichtman. *Current Health 2* v. 33 pp12–15 October 2006.

Global hunger remains a serious problem, Lichtman demonstrates. According to the UN, world hunger rates have risen in recent years, and hunger rose at a rate of almost 4 million people per year in the late 1990s. The UN claims that these rises are due to nations that are not investing enough in farming. In addition, war can make growing and obtaining food difficult. Going without food can result in brain damage, stunted growth, and learning disabilities. Moreover, the Hunger Project, an organization that works to end world hunger, claims that approximately 24,000 people a day die from hunger-related problems.

Southern Africa: From Hand to Mouth. *The Economist* v. 377 pp55–56 October 8, 2005.

The crucial rains of January, when newly planted crops need water, did not come on time in 2005, *The Economist* reports, and food prices in markets have increased beyond the means of the hungriest people. The problem is a recurring one across southern Africa, where food is produced mainly on small plots with no irrigation by subsistence farmers, whose fate is tied to rain falling in the right amount at the right time.

How Freer Trade Can Help Feed the Poor. John Nash and Donald Mitchell. *Finance & Development* v. 42 p34–37 March 2005.

Nash and Mitchell argue that global trade liberalization is one of the weapons in the arsenal to fight the world's hunger problem and can make an important contribution by delivering cheaper food in protectionist countries and boosting the global economy, thus helping to lift millions out of poverty. The writers examine how trade policy can be harnessed to help reduce poverty and alleviate hunger and outline an agenda to reduce food insecurity in developing countries.

The World's Water Crisis. Clifton Coles. *The Futurist* v. 39 p14 March/April 2005.

Conservation and creative capitalism could ensure the continued availability of water, Coles writes. According to Robin Clarke and Jannet King, the authors of *The Water Atlas*, radical measures are required to change the way water is sourced, used, and managed in order to avoid a severe water shortage. They claim the water crisis will probably result in ecological damage and limit food production severely, causing malnutrition and disease. They argue that water management that takes a holistic view and involves the communities using the water is vital to maintaining the world's water health, as is finance for research to develop water-conservation technologies and cooperation between countries sharing river basins.

Making Famine History. Cormac Ó Gráda. *The Journal of Economic Literature* v. 45 pp5–38 March 2007.

Ó Gráda discusses recent contributions to the economics and economic history of famine. After reviewing alternative explanations for why famines occur and persist, the writer addresses the problems associated with defining and identifying famines and highlights some methodological issues that arise in studying them. Ó Gráda maintains that although the demographic cost of famines has undoubtedly been reduced as a result of material progress and developments in medical technology, their long-term cost in terms of health may be greater than previously thought. He then discusses three of the most important and controversial famines of the 20th century: the Soviet famine of 1932–33, the Bengali famine of 1942–44, and the Chinese famine of 1959–61.

New Variant Famine: AIDS and Food Crisis in Southern Africa. Alex De Waal and Alan Whiteside. *Lancet (North American edition)* v. 362 pp1234–37 October 11, 2003.

The authors propose that the southern African food crisis can be attributed largely to the HIV/AIDS epidemic in the region. They present evidence that the region is facing a new variant famine, using frameworks drawn from famine theory to examine the implications. HIV/AIDS has created a new category of highly vulnerable households—namely, those with ill adults or those whose adults have died. The general burden of care in both AIDS-affected and non-AIDS-affected households has reduced the viability of farming livelihoods. The sensitivity of rural communities to external shocks such as drought has increased, and their resilience has declined. The prospects for a sharp decline into severe famine are increased, and possibilities for recovery reduced.

Sowing Seeds of Revolt. Alex Gillis. *Maclean's* v. 120 p53 April 2, 2007.

Bill Gates's green revolution has been shunned by many Africans, Gillis reports. The Alliance for a Green Revolution in Africa, beginning with a $150 million fund that will develop 400 varieties of high-yielding seeds in sub-Saharan Africa, was launched in September 2006. The effort, which aims to eliminate hunger for 30 million to 40 million people, is inspired by the first green revolution, which started about 60 years ago, spreading high-yielding seeds, pesticides, and fertilizers to increase crop yields in Asia and Latin America. Hundreds of African farming organizations want nothing to do with Gates's program, however; Mamadou Goita, a development socio-economist in Mali, has explained that these groups want control of their own seeds and livelihoods.

Take Action: Support a Better Farm Bill. Willie Nelson. *The Mother Earth News* p85 June/July 2007.

Family farmers have always understood the direct link between healthy soil, food, and people, taking great measures to improve and protect their soil, Nelson writes. The key to strengthening this fabric that holds the United States together is to keep family farmers on the land. This also offers a solution to many of today's most pressing concerns: climate change, fossil fuel dependence, childhood obesity, and declining biodiversity. In the coming months, Congress will pass the next farm bill, which is so broad in scope that it touches food, renewable energy, nutrition, environmental stewardship, and hunger. Over the past several decades, the legislation has, however, served the interests of large-scale industrial agriculture with policies designed to produce cheap food and plenty of it. The result has been a depleted countryside with fewer farmers, degraded soils and waterways, and public health disasters. Nelson calls for a new farm bill, one that serves the interests of all Americans.

Flour Power. Kate Rounds. *Ms.* v. 12 p68 Spring 2002.

Rounds discusses the idea of the UN World Food Program (WFP) to give food to women as better insurance that families will be fed. According to Catherine Bertini, executive director of the WFP, if hunger is to end, partnerships with women must be formed, because men sell food rather than cook it, and the money does not go back into households for food. She has harnessed the resources of a $1.7 billion budget to tackle the gargantuan mandate of feeding the hungry of the world. The 7 million hungry in Afghanistan were a WFP priority, and the program has funded 157 bakeries in Kabul, of which 25 are run by women.

A Right to Food? How to Frame the Fight Against Hunger. Frances Moore Lappe. The Nation v. 283 pp39–40 September 11, 2006.

Lappe examines the pros and cons of legally establishing the right to food and argues that a more basic frame for addressing hunger might be through the empowerment of citizens to create strong communities.

Children as Barter in a Famished Land. Barry Bearak. *The New York Times (Late New York Edition)* pA1+ March 8, 2002.

After selling his farm animals, rugs, then cooking utensils, Akhtar Muhammad took two of his 10 children to the bazaar and traded them for bags of wheat. Others in the village of Kangori in Afghanistan's Sar-i-Pol Province forage for wild spinach and bitter grass that can be eaten if boiled long enough. After four years of drought, famine has gripped the country, and while mass starvation has been avoided, millions have been left malnourished and small pockets of starvation remain, Bearak reports. Even without famine, after two decades of war, statistically one in five children dies before age 5 and life expectancy is 44.

In Congo, Hunger and Disease Erode Democracy. Lydia Polgreen. *The New York Times (Late New York Edition)* pA1+ June 23, 2006.

Continuous fighting and political uncertainty have cast doubts over Congo's democratic future, Polgreen writes. While the country is headed towards its first free elections since 1965, more and more refugees appear, plagued by hunger, violence, and diseases.

Niger's Anguish Is Reflected in Its Dying Children. Michael Wines. *The New York Times (Late New York Edition)* ppA1+ August 5, 2005.

Niger's current famine is a result of droughts, poor social conditions, and long-standing international neglect, Wines writes. Children are being hit the hardest; out of 1,000 infants 262 will not reach the age of five. Experts emphasize that media attention will result in short-term relief, but that Niger's problems demand long-term commitment.

Why People Still Starve. Barry Bearak. *The New York Times Magazine* pp32+ July 13, 2003.

The World Food Program estimates that almost 40 million Africans are struggling against starvation, an unprecedented number. Coincident with the hunger is HIV/AIDS, which has resulted in 29.4 million infections in sub-Saharan Africa, almost three-quarters of the world's caseload. African nations now make up the 27 lowest places on the human-development index—a combined measure of health, literacy, and income calculated by the UN—and they hold 38 positions in the bottom 50. Bearak discusses the suffering that has been caused by widespread food shortages in the African nation of Malawi.

The "Hunger Season." Eric Pape. *Newsweek* v. 146 p30 August 15, 2005.

Despite rain coming to drought-affected Niger and the arrival of hundreds of tons of famine relief, 160,000 of the country's children are suffering from serious malnutrition, and the lives of 32,000 are in immediate danger. August is known as the "hunger season" in Niger, a time when all the grain has been eaten and the autumn harvest has yet to start. Pape relates that in 2005, food became scarce long before August.

How to Cut World Hunger in Half. Per Lindskog. *Science* v. 310 p1768 December 16, 2005.

To help considerably reduce world hunger, wealthy countries must accept free-trade principles in their trade with developing countries, Lindskog argues. Whereas rich countries donate $1 billion per annum in agricultural aid to developing countries, they subsidize agriculture in their own countries with almost $1 billion per day. At the World Trade Organization negotiations in Hong Kong in December 2005, Lindskog asserts, developed countries must agree to greatly reduce their support for domestic agriculture, prohibit export subsidies, and considerably lower barriers to exports from developing countries. In contrast to the impact of aid and debt cancellation, the money from the higher prices for agricultural produce from developing countries goes directly to the poorest people and farmers in those countries.

World Poverty and Hunger: The Challenge for Science. Ismail Serageldin. *Science* v. 296 pp54–58 April 5, 2002.

Serageldin explores the global revolution brought about by numerous scientific advances. In the world that will emerge from this revolution, science has the potential to have both positive and negative effects. New and profound ethical and safety issues are being raised by mankind's new capacities, and new issues of proprietary science complicate the future. The paradox of the times is that a world of plenty, dazzling scientific advances, and technological breakthroughs continues to be marred by conflict, violence, economic uncertainty, and tragic poverty. If science is to realize its full potential and become the primary force for change in the world, scientists must engage scientific research in the pressing issues of our time: abolishing hunger and reducing poverty; promoting a scientific outlook and the values of science; and building real partnerships with scientists in the developing world.

Students Support the Millennium Development Goals. Faye Neville. *UN Chronicle* v. 43 pp29–30 March/May 2006.

Neville reports that young people worldwide are working to support the Millennium Development Goals (MDGs), thanks to the UN, the 2005 Live8 concert, MTV, and some international celebrities. In 2000, governments committed themselves to a global partnership, promising to accomplish the eight MDGs by 2015: eradicate extreme poverty and hunger; achieve universal primary education for all boys and girls; promote gender equality and empower women; reduce by two-thirds the mortality rate of children under five; reduce by three-quarters the ratio of maternal mortality; ensure environmental sustainability; develop a global partnership for development; and combat HIV/AIDS, malaria, and other diseases. Young people's support for the MDGs requires a multitude of actions, from holding governments accountable for more fair trade, debt aid, and cancellation of relief to writing letters, developing partnerships across the world, and raising money.

Revisiting Ireland's Great Famine. Nell Boyce. *U.S. News & World Report* v. 130 pp44–45 June 18, 2005.

Boyce discusses researchers' efforts, using genetic tests on 150-year-old leaf samples, to identify the source of the potato blight that caused Ireland's devastating famine of the 1840s. Scientists once thought that the blight originated in Mexico and that one strain of the disease—US-1—spread from there to America and Europe in the 19th century, but a recent report in *Nature* suggests otherwise. DNA research conducted by Jean Ristaino of North Carolina State University in Raleigh found that the epidemic was not caused by US-1.

She and her colleagues are now carrying out DNA tests on hundreds of other specimens from the period in an effort to pinpoint the disease's source, which she suspects is South America. Scientists are keen to locate the pest's origin because they might then be able to find wild plants that have lived long enough with the disease to develop strong resistance and to breed genes from those plants into modern potatoes to help combat the global resurgence of blight.

In Battling Hunger, a New Advance: Peanut-Butter Paste. Roger Thurow. *Wall Street Journal (Eastern Edition)* ppA1+ April 12, 2005.

Thurow explores a new advance in battling hunger—a peanut-butter paste named Plumpy'nut. Developed by the French company Nutriset SAS, the paste does not use water, is easily distributed, and is now widely used to combat the current famine in Darfur, Sudan. Plumpy'nut's origins can be traced to the African hunger crises of the early 1980s.

The Hunger Experiment. Sharman Apt Russell. *The Wilson Quarterly* v. 29 pp66–82 Summer 2005.

In 1944 and 1945, American volunteers took part in starvation experiments conducted by a group of private citizens at the University of Minnesota's Laboratory of Physiological Hygiene. As part of what became known as the Minnesota experiment, several dozen U.S. conscientious objectors agreed to starve themselves under medical supervision in order to examine ways in which the health of starved populations could be restored after the war. Headed by Ancel Keys, the director of the lab, the experiments were partly funded by pacifist organizations, such as the American Society of Friends and the Brethren Service Committee. Russell discusses the experiments and reflects that the results reveal a great deal about the problem of hunger, which currently afflicts approximately 800 million people worldwide.

Africa's Famine: No Shortage of Blame. *World Press Review* v. 50 pp22–25 April 2003.

Solutions to the problem of possible widespread starvation in southern Africa are few, and fault is widespread, this article states. As of 2003, an estimated 38 million people throughout southern Africa were at grave risk of starvation. Drought, AIDS, poverty, conflict, politics, and the mismanagement of international aid contribute to this problem.

Index